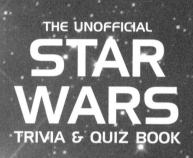

THE UNOFFICIAL

STAR
WARS
TRIVIA & QUIZ BOOK

THE UNOFFICIAL

STAR WARS

TRIVIA & QUIZ BOOK

A GALAXY OF MOVIE FUN FROM ANAKIN TO YODA

Mark Shulman

METRO BOOKS
NEW YORK

Interior design by Liz Travato

Metro Books
122 Fifth Avenue
New York, NY 1001

ISBN-13: 978-1-4351-0656-7

ISBN-10: 1-4351-0656-3

Printed and bound in the United States of America

1 3 5 7 9 10 8 6 4 2

For Alan and the expert staff at
Alan's Alley Video Store in Chelsea, NYC.
They really, really know what they're talking about.

Acknowledgments

First and foremost, I would like to thank my editorial director, Celeste Sollod, for her tremendous support and invaluable insights. She knows I approached this job like Luke approaching the Death Star, and we got explosive results. Vast thanks also to Hazlitt Krog, my occasional writing partner, for being an irreplaceable sounding board during critical times, and to his stunning wife Alexia, even after the Anakin wristwatch imbroglio on the opening day of TPM. Thanks to Sylvian Despretz, Henry Hollander, and the editorial staff at *Gort Magazine* for giving me a start. Most importantly, my undying gratitude to my unbelievably patient wife, Kara, who wasn't a *Star Wars* fan in her youth, but has learned to tolerate (if not appreciate) that every single analogy, simile, and metaphor on Earth can be applied somehow to the *Star Wars* universe. It really can, you know. I'll try to keep it under control from now on. And of course, thanks to you for picking up this book and reading this far.

P.S. My gratitude to anyone who has ever contributed to Wookieepedia. And isn't that name just perfect?

THE ANSWERS

About This Book

What you hold in your hand is a powerful testament to the imagination of George Lucas.

The Unofficial Star Wars Trivia & Quiz Book has been lovingly created for the casual fan and the ardent fanatic alike. You may find some questions easy, and some impossible, but nearly all the questions can be answered by simply watching the movies. Very few questions require any knowledge of the *Star Wars* Extended Universe that lives only in the literature beyond the films. Even then, if you didn't know it before, you'll enjoy what you learn.

The book has been divided into 33 chapters spanning all six films, with some emphasis on the original trilogy. The questions are generally distributed from the oldest film to the newest. Next to most of the questions, you will find a three-letter code that's actually the initials of the film where the answer can be found.

First Trilogy Films

ANH	*Star Wars IV*:	*A New Hope* (1977)
ESB	*Star Wars V*:	*The Empire Strikes Back* (1980)
ROJ	*Star Wars VI*:	*Return of the Jedi* (1983)

Second Trilogy Films

TPM	*Star Wars I*:	*The Phantom Menace* (1999)
AOC	*Star Wars II*:	*Attack of the Clones* (2002)
ROS	*Star Wars III*:	*Revenge of the Sith* (2005)

If a question hasn't got a three-letter code, then either the code would have been a giveaway, or the question didn't specifically relate to any one film.

Where a question asks you for a chronological answer, it relates to time within the film's universe, and isn't based on the year a film came out. Therefore, events in *Revenge of the Sith* occur chronologically before those in *A New Hope*, even though ROS was released 28 years after ANH. Now, how many *Star Wars* years passed between the two films? How old was Luke at the beginning of ANH? 19 years.

Every effort has been made to ensure the accuracy of these answers. The shooting scripts and the DVD subtitles were used to confirm spellings and plot points. Forays onto StarWars.com and Wookieepedia have confirmed and informed the answers. Any trivia gleaned from an unofficial source was double-checked against other materials before it was added to this book.

Meet Mark Shulman

And who am I, you ask? Back in 1977, on a certain film's opening day, I was the kid at the head of the line of the first matinee in my home-town. Perhaps I forgot to go to school that day, but I remembered to give the newspaper reporter my real name. Somehow I survived the ensuing fracas to see *Star Wars* (no Roman numeral then) many more times that summer.

I am the author of 90-plus books, for children and adults, with titles like *The Brainiac Box: 600 Things Every Smart Person Should Know* and *Mom and Dad are Palindromes* and *Attack of the Killer Video Book* and *The Voodoo Revenge Book*.

When I think about my original collection of *Star Wars* comics, posters, trading cards, novels, calendars, books, film stills, and toys, and the hundreds of hours spent in conversation and contemplation of the first film alone, words like *enjoyment* and *fulfillment* come to mind. As an adult, I can't help but also think about the word *vindication*.

You see, Mom? I told you I was doing it all for a reason.

The Questions

Anakin Skywalker

1. What was Anakin Skywalker's first line of dialog, and in what language was it? TPM
2. What was the first thing Anakin ever asked Padmé? TPM
3. Who accompanied young Anakin to meet his mother, and why did they come visit? TPM
4. Who was Anakin's father? TPM
5. What was Anakin's mother's name? TPM
6. What were the results of Anakin's blood test? TPM
7. Who was Anakin's young friend who explained that Anakin had never finished a race? TPM
8. Where did Anakin first hear the phrase, "May the Force be with you"? TPM
9. How did Anakin end up initially taking the lead from Sebulba in the pod race? TPM
10. How did Anakin's mother respond when a departing Anakin said, "I don't want things to change"? TPM
11. Where exactly did Anakin Skywalker meet Obi-Wan Kenobi?
12. Who first explained the dark side of the Force to Anakin?
13. What was the first sentence that Palpatine spoke to Anakin?

The role of the adult Anakin was finally cast after about 3,000 actors were considered for the part.

14. What was Anakin wearing when he was last seen in TPM?

15. Why did Anakin say he was sweating on the elevator in AOC?

16. What did Obi-Wan say would happen if his very young apprentice spent as much time practicing saber techniques as he spent practicing his wit? AOC

17. Anakin explained to Padmé on the starfreighter in AOC that two aspects of love were forbidden to a Jedi, but a third was central to a Jedi's life. What were the three aspects?

18. Where did Anakin first kiss Padmé?

19. When Anakin described "aggressive negotiations" with Padmé, what did he explain that to mean? AOC

20. What did Anakin see in the nightmare he described to Padmé? AOC

21. How did Anakin's lightsaber get destroyed on Geonosis? AOC

22. What got lost as a result of Anakin's first amputation?

23. What color prosthesis did Anakin get at the end of AOC?

24. Who were the two witnesses in Anakin and Padmé's wedding? AOC

Ken Annakin, a film director and friend to George Lucas, provided the name. In Sanskrit, the word means warrior.

25. What did General Grievous tell Anakin he expected of someone with Anakin's reputation? ROS

26. What command did Anakin give in order to help land the Trade Federation cruiser as it plummeted toward Coruscant? ROS

27. In ROS, Anakin looked at a pendant around Padmé's neck and said he remembered where he gave it to her. Where and when did he give it to her?

28. Under what condition did Mace Windu allow Anakin to sit on the Jedi Council? ROS

29. Anakin said the Jedi Council's request to spy on Palpatine was against four things. What?

30. Did Anakin actually fulfill the prophecy of the Chosen One?

31. With what words did Anakin declare himself to become a Sith Lord?

32. What did Anakin do immediately after Mace died? ROS

33. What was Anakin's last act as a husband? ROS

34. Exactly which injuries did Darth Vader sustain on Mustafar? ROS

35. Why did Anakin want Luke to take off his mask at the end of ROJ?

36. What were Anakin Skywalker's last words as he died?

The Bad Guys

Sith Lords add "Darth" to their name as a commitment to the dark side of the Force. "Darth" is usually seen as a contraction of the title "Dark Lord of the Sith."

1. Who killed Uncle Owen and Aunt Beru? ANH
2. What were Tarkin's two titles on the Death Star? ANH
3. The Tusken Raider who attacked Luke had how many spiked objects on top of his head? ANH
4. Who or what did Tarkin say had been "dissolved"? ANH
5. What were the names of the three green Neimoidian leaders of the Trade Federation? TPM
6. How did Lord Sidious refer to the Neimoidian captain at the beginning of TPM?
7. What was the name of the place where Viceroy Nute told the battle droid to process the Queen and her party? TPM
8. Where exactly did we first see Darth Maul? TPM
9. What color lighting was inside Darth Maul's ship? TPM
10. How many probe droids did Darth Maul employ on Tatooine? TPM
11. How many times did Darth Maul blink during TPM?
12. What were the Tusken Raiders doing when they were introduced in TPM?
13. How many Sith were there at any time, according to Yoda?
14. What was the first name of the secret agent who was hired to kill Padmé in AOC?
15. Who hired the assassin to kill Padmé? AOC

16. How was the son of the original host of the clone army believed to have died? AOC

17. Whom did Jango Fett say recruited him, and where was he recruited? AOC

18. What did Jango Fett use to attack Obi-Wan's ship in the chase in the asteroid field? AOC

19. Who said he wouldn't sign a treaty until he had Padmé's head on his desk? AOC

20. Which council, which clan, and which federation agreed to sign Count Dooku's treaty? AOC

21. What was Count Dooku's first line of dialog?

22. What had been Count Dooku's career before we met him in AOC?

23. Who captured Anakin on Geonosis? AOC

24. How did Jango Fett die?

25. What was Boba Fett's last action in AOC?

26. In AOC, at the beginning of Clone Wars, the Geonosian Archduke Poggle the Lesser (the guy with the face like a squid) said that the Jedi must not find something that he had. What?

27. Who was billed as the "fiendish droid leader" in the opening text of ROS?

28. According to the opening text of ROS, where are the heroes and where is the evil?

29. What were crawling around General Grievous's ship in the opening battle sequence of ROS?

30. How many battle droids were passengers on the command ship elevator in which Obi-Wan and Anakin hid?

31. What command from General Grievous caused the plummeting Trade Federation cruiser to level out in ROS?

32. What was Dooku's command ship's elevator's number, and what happened to its roof? ROS

33. What were the last words Count Dooku heard?

34. With Dooku dead, who became the leader of the droid army?

35. Where did Darth Sidious suggest that Grievous move the Separatist leaders? ROS

36. Where did Yoda say General Grievous was hiding? ROS

37. What was the Sith legend of Darth Plaegueis?

38. What happened to Darth Plaegueis?

39. What was General Grievous hiding beneath his cold, hard robotic shell? ROS

40. How did General Grievous die? ROS

41. Who carried out Darth Sidious's order to kill all the Jedi? ROS

42. Who was sent to prepare Darth Sidious's shuttle for immediate takeoff in ROS?

Behind the Scenes

1. Whom did George Lucas name Anakin for?
2. What 10 Academy Award nominations did ANH get in 1977, and which did it win?
3. What three Academy Award nominations did ESB get in 1980, and which did it win?
4. What was the ranking of *Star Wars* among the American Film Institute's Top 100 films of all time?
5. You probably know which *Star Wars* character was named to the American Film Institute's Top 50 Villains list, but what was his ranking?

A partial list of who auditioned:

Nick Nolte = Han Solo
John Travolta = Han Solo
Christopher Walken = Han Solo
Burt Reynolds = turned down Han Solo*
Amy Irving = Princess Leia
Karen Allen = Princess Leia
Jodie Foster = Princess Leia
Cindy Williams = Princess Leia
William Katt = Luke Skywalker
Dennis Dugan = Luke Skywalker
Toshiro Mifune = Obi-Wan Kenobi
Orson Welles = Darth Vader's voice

* But Reynolds appeared in the unforgettable *Smoky and the Bandit*, which opened the same weekend as *Star Wars*.

6. Which *Star Wars* quote is listed among the American Film Institute's Top 100 Movie Quotes?

7. Which two *Star Wars* heroes were named to the American Film Institute's Top 50 Heroes list, and what was their ranking?

8. Which recurring *Star Wars* actor said, "Actually, I really wanted to play Princess Leia. Stick some big pastries on my head. Now, that would be interesting."

9. Why did George Lucas have the Wampa snow beast in ESB harm Luke's face on Hoth?

10. What caused the destructive pile-up of R2-D2 and other remote-control robots during the filming of ANH in Tunisia?

11. Which notable figures played the two Imperial commandos who lost control of the AT-PT when it was taken over by Chewbacca and the two Ewoks? ROJ

12. What did George Lucas finally admit was the process by which he came up with R2-D2's name?

13. What dubious financial feat did AOC accomplish?

14. Who wore the Vader suit at the end of ROS?

15. What was the original working title of *Return of the Jedi*?

16. How many of the six films were nominated for Best Visual Effects Oscars?

17. The Roman numeral IV and the name *A New Hope* got added to the original film *Star Wars* after the release of which other film?

18. How was James Earl Jones originally credited in the 1977 release of ANH?

19. Which famous film director wrote (or co-wrote, depending on your source) the opening text of ANH?

20. In which years was ANH re-released theatrically?

21. What was born when George Lucas observed a hamburger with an olive next to it?

22. Why didn't Lucas want Harrison Ford to audition for Han Solo?
23. In which film was "The Imperial March" (Darth Vader's theme) introduced?
24. In how many movie theatres did ANH get released originally?
25. Which Star Wars actor is the real-life nephew of the actor who played Wedge Antilles?
26. What was the wardrobe malfunction that affected all the Imperial military uniforms in ROJ, but would have been too expensive to repair in post-production?
27. What did George Lucas say was uncommon about the narrative arc of ESB?
28. Which two famous directors named David reportedly turned down the chance to direct ROJ?
29. Who was George Lucas's first choice to direct ROJ?
30. How did the film Blue Harvest have anything to do with ROJ?
31. What was the surprise awaiting David Prowse at the end of ROJ?
32. Why did the Dagobah set have to be raised off the ground several feet?
33. What ranking did John Williams's musical score to Star Wars receive on the American Film Institute's list of the greatest film scores of all time?
34. What happened on the second day of filming in the Tunisian desert that hadn't happened there in 50 years? ANH
35. Which was the only Star Wars film to use locations in the United States?
36. Where were George Lucas and his crew located while Mark Hamill was climbing through snow to escape the abominable Wampa?

C-3PO

1. Chronologically, what were C-3PO's first lines of dialog? TPM
2. After introducing himself, what was the first thing R2-D2 said to C-3PO?
3. What insult did R2-D2 hurl at C-3PO because the golden droid wouldn't get into the escape pod at the beginning of ANH?
4. What did C-3PO have to say about Princess Leia's ship as he and R2-D2 jettisoned away in the escape pod? ANH
5. What convinced C-3PO to get into the escape pod with R2-D2? ANH
6. What affliction did C-3PO say was affecting him while in the Tatooine desert? ANH
7. What did C-3PO wonder to R2-D2 about what the Jawas would do to them? ANH
8. C-3P0 was fluent in over how many forms of communication?
9. What did C-3PO say had been his first job? ANH
10. As C-3PO was lowered into his oil bath, he thanked someone. Who? ANH
11. What command did Luke give to C3PO to give to R2-D2 to stop the trash compactor? ANH
12. Where did C-3PO say he wanted to take the over-excited, over-run R2-D2 as he fooled the guard on the Death Star hangar bay? ANH
13. What did C-3PO offer to donate to R2-D2 at the end of the Battle of Yavin? ANH

14. When C-3PO told Han that Luke was missing in ESB, whom did Han call out for?

15. What insult did C-3PO hurl at R2-D2 after telling him that the missing Luke would be quite all right? ESB

16. Why did C-3PO say that Master Luke was quite clever? ESB

17. What did C-3PO keep trying to tell Han as they escaped Hoth on the Millennium Falcon, but Han wouldn't listen? ESB

18. What are the odds of successfully navigating an asteroid field, according to C-3PO?

19. According to C-3PO, what are the odds of surviving a direct assault on an Imperial Star Destroyer? ESB

20. What did C-3PO think R2-D2 would do if the shorter droid heard half of what C-3PO knows about Jabba? ROJ

21. How did C-3PO announce the droids' arrival at Jabba's palace? ROJ

22. How did C-3PO say, "We've come to see Jabba the Hutt" in Huttese. ROJ

23. Where in Jabba's palace did C-3PO get assigned to work? ROJ

24. What did C-3PO say he couldn't bear to watch? ROJ

25. What did Han tell C-3PO to use to get his Rebel team freed from the Ewoks? ROJ

26. What did C-3PO say to R2-D2 after Han told him to stay in the woods rather than approach the control bunker? ROJ

27. What did C-3PO call "perverse" while visiting Geonosis? AOC

28. Who or what did C-3PO end up exchanging heads with? AOC

C-3PO was based on the robot Maria in Fritz Lang's 1927 film masterpiece *Metropolis*.

29. What did C-3PO say about his programming as he discovered his new body marching into the Geonosis arena for battle?
30. What was Bail Organa's final command regarding C-3PO? ROS
31. Which famous movie character voice actor auditioned for the part of C-3PO?

C-3PO had several owners onscreen. Anakin was his maker, then he was owned by Anakin's mother, Shmi; her husband, Cliegg Lars; Padmé; several others offscreen; then Captain Antilles; Owen Lars; Luke Skywalker; Jabba the Hutt; Luke again; and, after ROJ, he went to Leia.

Chewbacca

1. The sounds of what animals were mixed to make Chewbacca's famous growl?
2. How did Peter Mayhew come to George Lucas's attention?
3. What species was Chewbacca, and how is it spelled?
4. What were Chewbacca's two main roles on the Millennium Falcon?
5. How tall was Chewbacca?
6. What was the species of the being who introduced Obi-Wan to Chewbacca in the cantina? ANH
7. On which shoulder did Chewbacca wear his ammunition belt in ANH?
8. What did Chewbacca bump his head against as he sat down in the Millennium Falcon for the first time? ANH

Peter Mayhew had the shortest audition for *Star Wars*: He stood up to greet George Lucas, and at 7 feet 2 inches, he was hired.

9. How many monsters were seen on the hologram game Chewbacca played with R2-D2? ANH

10. According to Han, what did Wookiees do when they lost a game? ANH

11. On the Millennium Falcon, what did Chewbacca lock in to keep it from the Death Star's tractor beam? ANH

12. What did Chewbacca try to do to keep the first TIE fighter they encountered near Alderaan from identifying the Millennium Falcon? ANH

13. What was Chewbacca wearing when he was first seen in ESB?

14. What tool did Han ask Chewbacca to bring him as the Millennium Falcon was stalled in space near Hoth? ESB

15. What did Han call Chewbacca when the Wookiee laughed at Han in Luke's medical room?

After the Chewbacca suit got wet in the garbage compactor scene, it reportedly smelled bad for the rest of the filming.

16. After the Millennium Falcon fled the space slug, what did Chewbacca say caused the problem with the ship's hyper-drive? ESB

17. What mistake did Chewbacca make while rebuilding C-3PO? ESB

18. What did the little ugnaughts do when Chewbacca tried to get the pieces of C-3PO back from them in Lando's junk room? ESB

19. How did Chewbacca finally get C-3PO's head back from Lando's ugnaughts? ESB

20. How much did Jabba offer to pay for Chewbacca? ROJ

21. Why was Chewbacca complaining when he sat down in the cockpit of the stolen Imperial shuttle? ROJ
22. What was Han's advice to Chewbacca on how to keep his distance without looking like he was keeping his distance? ROJ
23. What did Chewbacca do to cause the first stormtrooper on Endor to fall off on his speeder bike? ROJ
24. How were the two Imperial soldiers operating an Imperial walker relieved of their job by Chewbacca and two Ewoks? ROJ
25. In which prequel trilogy film does Chewbacca appear?
26. On what actual living creature was Chewbacca based on? (And for bonus points, what other blockbuster film character's name was also based on that same dog?)
27. How did Han Solo and Chewbacca meet? (For experts only—never filmed.)

Darth Vader

1. What were Anakin's first words as Darth Vader?

2. Which two people were strangled by Darth Vader in ANH?

3. When the Millennium Falcon was identified on the Death Star as a ship that left Tatooine, what did Darth Vader correctly assume? ANH

4. When Darth Vader first encountered the Millennium Falcon in ANH, he said he felt a presence he had not felt since when?

5. Darth Vader said that something was not Obi-Wan's plan on the Death Star. What? ANH

6. What were Darth Vader's first words to Obi-Wan on the Death Star? ANH

7. How does Darth Vader characterize Obi-Wan's powers in ANH?

8. Why did Darth Vader say a certain day would be "a day long remembered"? ANH

9. Why, in fact, was the day "long remembered"? ANH

10. What was notable about Darth Vader's electronic breastplate during his duel with Obi-Wan? ANH

11. What did Darth Vader do immediately after Obi-Wan's body vanished after their duel on the Death Star? ANH

12. Why was Darth Vader confused about Obi-Wan becoming a Force ghost on the Death Star? ANH

13. How did Darth Vader identify the Rebel attackers he decided to personally fight in space? ANH

14. What was Darth Vader obsessed with, according to the opening text in ESB?

15. By what means did Darth Vader find Luke in the Galaxy? ESB

16. What was the color scheme of Darth Vader's spherical meditation cubicle?

17. What did we first see, for a moment, inside Vader's meditation cubicle? ESB

18. What else, besides Vader himself, was visible inside Darth Vader's egg-like meditation cubicle? ESB

19. What did Darth Vader say was Admiral Ozzel's "clumsy, stupid" error? ESB

20. What was Darth Vader's first line of dialog with the Emperor in ESB?

21. How did Darth Vader stop Han's laser blasts when they first met in the Cloud City?

22. With what words did Darth Vader greet Han for the first time in ESB?

23. Why did Darth Vader have Han Solo frozen in carbonite? ESB

24. What did Darth Vader first say to Luke the first time they met?

25. What did Darth Vader tell Luke was his destiny in ESB, as foreseen by the Emperor?

26. In ESB, who drew his lightsaber first: Luke or Darth Vader?

27. How did Luke and Darth Vader each go down the same staircase at the beginning of their ESB duel?

28. In what film do you see the inside of Darth Vader's mask?

29. Did Darth Vader encounter the droid he built in TPM any time in the original trilogy?

30. In order to keep the ending of ESB a secret, actor David Prowse was told to say what to Luke instead of "I am your father"?

31. What did Darth Vader say was his purpose for arriving at the second Death Star? ROJ

32. What was Vader's response when Commander Jerjerrod said that his men were working as fast as they could to complete the second Death Star? ROJ

33. What was the first thing Darth Vader said to the Emperor in ROJ?

34. Why were Luke and Leia hidden from Darth Vader, according to Obi-Wan?

35. What did the Emperor tell Darth Vader would be Luke's undoing? ROJ

36. In what scene did Darth Vader purposefully save Chewbacca's life?

37. What was Darth Vader's first comment to Luke above Endor? ROJ

38. What did Darth Vader observe about Luke when he saw Luke had constructed a new lightsaber? ROJ

39. What was Darth Vader's reply when Luke said he wouldn't turn, and that Vader would be forced to kill him? ROJ

40. What did Darth Vader do after he said, "If you will not fight, then you will meet your destiny"? ROJ

George Lucas said that the name Darth Vader was meant to sound like Dark Father. Vader means father in Dutch.

41. What did Han do after the last Imperial troops had been captured outside the command bunker on Endor? ROJ

42. How did Darth Vader discover that Luke had a sister? ROJ

43. What did Darth Vader do after Luke had (literally) disarmed him? ROJ

44. How did actor David Prowse learn that his spoken lines as Darth Vader had been dubbed over? ANH

45. Who provided the smooth baritone voice that was used to replace Prowse's as Darth Vader?

46. Who provided the voice of Darth Vader once he was put into his helmet in ROS?

47. What was Darth Vader's first question after he was encased in his famous black outfit? ROS

48. What was Darth Vader's last line of dialogue in ROS?

Darth Vader was not originally going to be a cyborg. The famous suit and mask were designed as Vader's space suit for boarding Leia's ship. The illustrations looked so good to Lucas that the suit became a key part of the character.

The Death Star

1. What were the two official roles of the two Death Stars?

2. What device on the Death Star pulled ships toward it?

3. What was most prominent on either Death Star's northern hemisphere?

4. How many smaller lasers from the first Death Star joined forces to create the single deadly blast that destroyed Alderaan? ANH

5. Who was commander of the first Death Star? ANH

6. What did the authorities on the Death Star announce they were doing to let the Millennium Falcon in? ANH

7. How did Luke and Han disguise themselves on the Death Star? ANH

8. When Han asked, "Could you give us a hand with this?" how many stormtroopers entered the Millennium Falcon? ANH

9. The stormtrooper whose armor Luke appropriated had which number? ANH

10. Luke claimed Chewbacca was a prisoner transfer from what cell block? ANH

11. What else, beside Imperial troops, did Han, Luke, and Chewbacca aim at when they first entered the detention area? ANH

12. What was Princess Leia's cell number? ANH

13. On what level of the Death Star was Princess Leia's detention block? ANH

14. What shape was the tunnel leading to Princess Leia's cell? ANH

15. What was the location number of the trash compactor that almost compacted Luke, Han, Leia, and Chewbacca? ANH

16. Which character discovered the location of the tractor beam's controls on the Death Star? ANH

17. What was written on the tractor beam that Obi-Wan disabled on the Death Star, and why are the words of interest? ANH

18. How many of the seven terminals would need to be disabled in order for the Death Star's tractor beam to free the Millennium Falcon?

19. At what speed was the Death Star said to be orbiting the planet Yavin? ANH

20. Who was the first Rebel pilot to fire missiles at the target on the Death Star? ANH

21. What was the last official order voiced on the original Death Star? ANH

22. What did the opening text in ROJ say the new Death Star would spell?

23. What protected the second, unfinished Death Star? ROJ

24. How many steps led up to the Emperor's seat at the large circular window in the Emperor's throne room on the Death Star? ROJ

25. How many smaller lasers from the second Death Star joined forces to create the single deadly blast that destroyed the Rebel cruiser? ROJ

26. Inside the Death Star, which power regulator did Lando order hit? ROJ

27. What color were the destructive lasers on the first and second Death Stars?

28. According to the Emperor, the second Death Star was, in fact, what? ROJ

29. Chronologically, where was the Death Star first seen on film?

The first Death Star has been estimated from 75 to 100 miles in diameter. The second was larger, with accounts ranging from 100 to 550 miles in diameter. Your results may vary.

Emperor Palpatine

1. "Henceforth you shall become known as _____"
2. Where did Palpatine first speak with Anakin?
3. What did Palpatine tell Anakin would follow when Anakin learned to trust his feelings?
4. When Anakin said to Palpatine that Obi-Wan's fate would be the same as theirs in ROS, how did that become true?
5. Who was the first person to verbally confirm that Darth Sidious was Palpatine?
6. In which two films did Palpatine sit and watch as his apprentice was about to be killed by the chosen successor (and say "Goooood")?
7. Upon arrival on the Death Star, the Emperor senses what in Darth Vader? ROJ
8. What did the Emperor tell Darth Vader to do once Luke sought out Vader, and why? ROJ
9. What did Obi-Wan and the Emperor each know about Anakin's children? ROJ
10. How did the Emperor reply when Darth Vader told him that Luke was among the rebels on Endor? ROJ
11. What were the Emperor's first words to Luke in his throne room on the Death Star? ROJ
12. According to the Emperor in his throne room, how exactly had everything "transpired"? ROJ

In ROJ, as the Rebels discussed attacking
the new Death Star, look for Ian McDiarmid
(The Emperor) in the crowd in the upper left corner
at the point when the Emperor was mentioned.

George Lucas had wanted to use the name Palatine, who was the character running for Senate in the film *Taxi Driver*, but lawyers persuaded him not to.

13. Who, said the Emperor, was walking into a trap? ROJ

14. The Emperor told Luke that the shield generator was safe from whom exactly? ROJ

15. In the final throne room scene in ROJ, what did the Emperor say Luke had paid the price for?

16. To how many Jedi knights did Palpatine say, "I can feel your anger"?

17. In which film(s) was Palpatine not seen or mentioned by any of his names?

18. In Palpatine's private chambers, to what special position did he appoint Anakin? ROS

19. How did Palpatine describe the special position? ROS

20. Palpatine convinced Anakin of what treasonous lie about the Jedi Council? ROS

21. In Palpatine's chambers, he suggested that Anakin do what to be "a complete and wise leader"? ROS

22. What did Palpatine accuse Mace and the other Jedi of when they came to arrest him? ROS

23. Who broke the panoramic window in Palpatine's chambers during his lightsaber battle with Mace Windu? ROS

24. What caused Palpatine's face to wither into the pale, wrinkled, grotesque one recognized as the Emperor's?

25. What was the name of Palpatine's official order to wipe out the Jedi? ROS

26. What were the Emperor's last words?

The Galactic Republic

1. According to Padmé, how does liberty die? ROS
2. What were the two official names of the Republic?
3. What did Qui-Gon call the "central system in the Republic"? TPM
4. What was the title of the leader of the Senate in the Republic?
5. According to the first paragraph of text at the beginning of TPM, why had turmoil engulfed the Galactic Republic?
6. Who secretly dispatched the Jedi Knights to settle the conflict? TPM
7. Meanwhile, what was the congress of the Republic reported to be doing to solve the turmoil? TPM
8. What was the name of the planet the Jedi Knights were dispatched to, and who was its ruler at the time? TPM
9. Which two figures appeared in the first two holographic transmissions in TPM?
10. What was the first line of dialog spoken inside the Republic's Senate chamber? TPM
11. What was the name of the ranking individual on Coruscant at the beginning of TPM?
12. Who took Valorum's job? AOC

Most of the known (and inhabited) Galaxy systems were members of the Galactic Republic, which stretched from the Core Worlds past the Outer Rim to the Wild Space.

13. Why was there unrest in the Galactic Senate, according to the opening text of AOC?

14. Who was named as the leader of the Separatist movement in the text at the beginning of AOC?

15. What legislation was being debated in AOC which Padmé did not want passed?

16. What was the official title of the Republic's plan to create a standing army? AOC

17. During a meeting with Naboo's Queen Jamillia, Padmé expressed her belief that the Separatists would turn for help to what groups if they felt threatened? AOC

18. What was the frustrating result of four trials against the Neimoidians in the Supreme Court? AOC

19. Which Senator introduced the motion to give Palpatine wide-ranging emergency powers? AOC

20. What was Palpatine's first action in the Galactic Senate, once given emergency powers? AOC

21. According to Queen Jamillia of Naboo, what happens on the day we stop believing democracy can work? AOC

22. Immediately after we saw Darth Vader with yellow Sith eyes in ROS, what did Palpatine announce to the Senate?

23. What political organization replaced the Galactic Senate? ROS

24. Chronologically, who is the first member of the Imperial Senate to appear onscreen?

The interplanetary Clone Wars lasted only three years, but ended with the death of the Galactic Republic and the creation of the Galactic Empire.

Han Solo

1. What was Han's first comment to Luke about Leia after having met her?

2. Where did Han Solo first meet Luke Skywalker?

3. How much did Han ask to be paid to take Obi-Wan and Luke to Alderaan? ANH

4. How much did Obi-Wan offer to pay Han and Chewbacca to go to Alderaan? ANH

5. What happened after Greedo shot first at Han Solo in the cantina in ANH?

6. How did Han first describe the wreckage of Alderaan that he encountered? ANH

7. What did Han say is no match for a blaster at your side? ANH

8. What exactly did Luke offer Han in order to get Han to help save Leia in ANH?

9. How much wealth can Han imagine? ANH

10. Han said attacking the Death Star wasn't courage, it was _____? ANH

11. What did Han say after he blasted the communications device on the Death Star's detention level? ANH

12. Why did Han's laser blast bounce all over the trash compactor? ANH

13. What convinced Han to leave the Rebellion and repay Jabba at the beginning of ESB?

14. What was the first sarcastic title Han directed at Leia in the frozen corridor just before she said "I thought you had decided to stay"? ESB

15. What happened after Han told the frozen Luke to give him a sign (of life)? ESB

Harrison Ford improvised Han Solo's conversation on the Death Star intercom to make his discomfort sound real.

16. What did Han have to say about the smell of tauntauns? ESB

17. How did Han keep Luke warm on the frozen surface of Hoth?

18. In the medical center on Hoth, Han said Luke looked strong enough to torment what animal how? ESB

19. In the medical center in ESB, Han told Luke, "That's two you owe me, Junior." What was the first?

20. What were Han's last words to Luke on Hoth? ESB

21. With what command to Chewbacca did Han fly into the asteroid field? ESB

22. When Leia told an advancing Han that she happened to like nice men, what did Han smoothly say? ESB

23. What did Han say first to Chewbacca after being tortured by Darth Vader in the Cloud City? ESB

24. What was the difference between Han's hands when he was lowered into the carbon freezing chamber and after he was frozen? ESB

25. How long, in years, had Han been frozen at the beginning of ROJ?

26. What was the name of the material that Han was frozen in?

27. When Han asked the bounty hunter in ROJ "Who are you?" what was the answer?

28. What did Han tell Jabba was the reason he hadn't paid Jabba back yet? ROJ

29. What was the main, temporary side effect of having been frozen in carbonite?

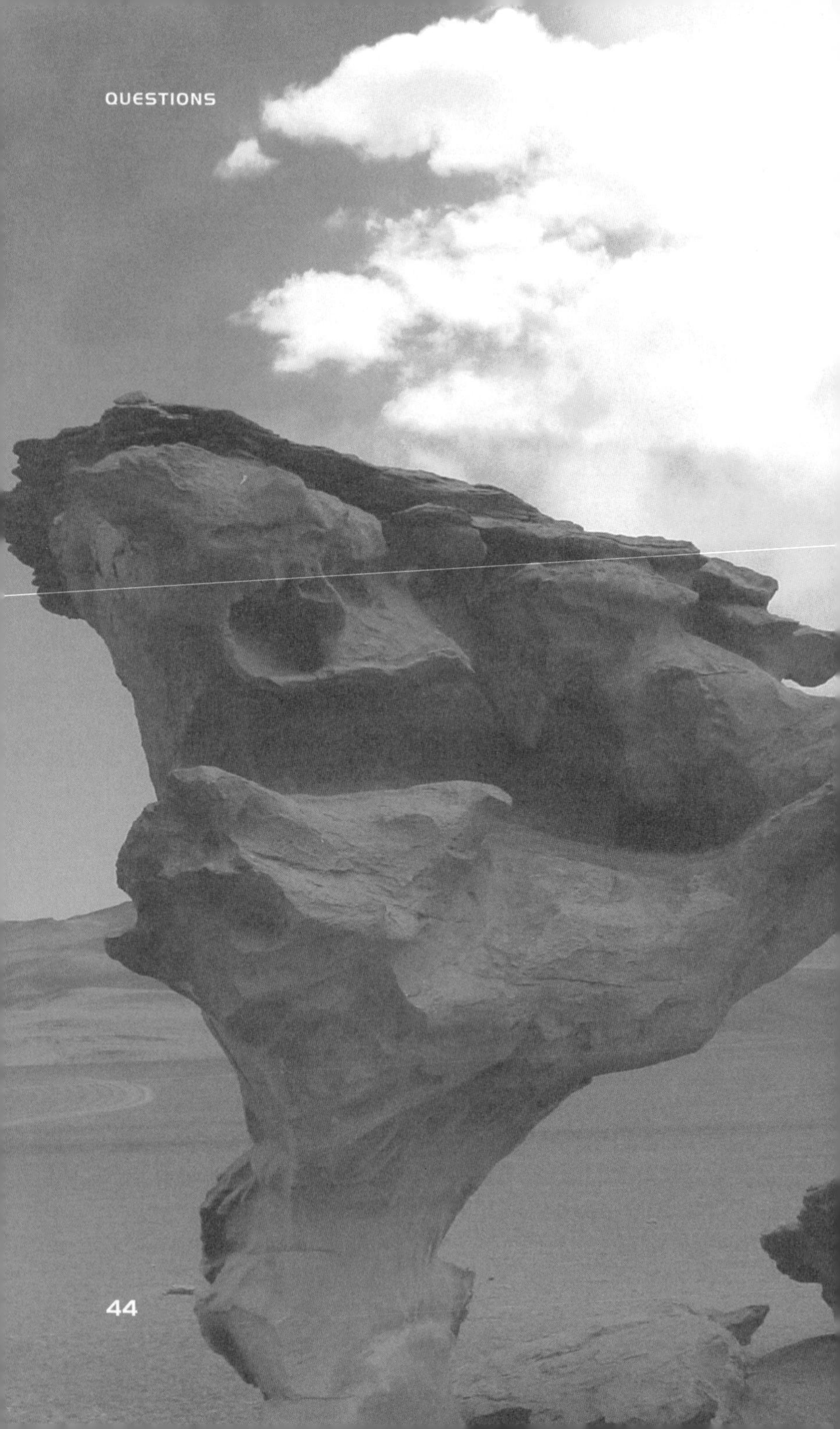

30. What was Han's reaction when he found out that Luke was now a Jedi knight? ROJ

31. What insult did Han aim at Jabba just before Han was to be thrown into the pit? ROJ

32. What rank did Han Solo receive before the Battle of Endor? ROJ

33. How did the Imperial stormtroopers on Endor realize that Han Solo was sneaking toward them? ROJ

34. What did the Ewok near Han Solo do while C-3PO acted out the first two *Star Wars* films in Ewokese? ROJ

35. What did the Imperial commander call Han as the Rebels were captured inside the control bunker on Endor? ROJ

36. How did Han ultimately open the door of the command bunker, after R2-D2 became damaged? ROJ

37. What happens to Han and Leia in the stories that take place after ROJ?

According to George Lucas, Han Solo was based on Francis Ford Coppola, except that Han was originally to be either a black man, or a green-skinned alien with gills but no nose.

Jabba the Hutt

1. Who was Jabba's bounty hunter in ANH?
2. Why did George Lucas remove the scene in ANH of Jabba confronting Han Solo until the 1997 re-release?
3. To whom did Darth Vader mention Jabba the Hutt for the first time?
4. Darth Vader said that Jabba could have Han Solo after what happened?
5. What color were Jabba's eyes? ROJ
6. In what order did C-3PO, Chewbacca, Han, Lando, Leia, Luke, and R2-D2 enter Jabba's palace in ROJ?
7. What did the thing that answered the door at Jabba's palace look like? ROJ
8. How did Luke address Jabba in the hologram projected by R2-D2? ROJ
9. What happened to the most recent protocol droid in Jabba's palace before C-3PO arrived? ROJ

The Jabba puppet in ROJ had four puppeteers: one controlled the voice, jaw, and right arm; one controlled the head, tongue, and left arm; another controlled the eyes; and the last one controlled the tail. Three puppeteers were inside the puppet during filming.

10. What was the name of the slave-girl dancer whom Jabba dropped through a trapdoor in ROJ?

11. What did Jabba do in his palace just after he sent the dancer through the trap door to her death? ROJ

12. What did Jabba do when C-3PO explained that the bounty hunter wanted 50,000 for Chewbacca? ROJ

13. What's the name of Jabba's pink, bumpy-headed, tentacle-shouldered assistant in ROJ?

14. What was the name of the giant fanged monster that lived in the pit beneath Jabba the Hutt? ROJ

15. What happened to the guard who found himself with Luke in the pit beneath Jabba? ROJ

16. How did the creatures in Jabba's court get the chance to watch the Rancor in action? ROJ

17. Jabba said in ROJ that Han may have been a good smuggler before, but now he was what?

18. How did Jabba die? ROJ

19. What was the name of Jabba the Hutt's sail barge?

20. What was the name of the little smirking birdlike creature who hovered around Jabba? ROJ

21. What animal did Jabba intend to employ to kill Luke, Leia, Han, and Chewbacca? ROJ

22. Who was billed in the credits of TPM as playing Jabba the Hutt?

Jar Jar Binks

1. What species was Jar Jar Binks?

2. What reason did Jar Jar Binks use for staying and becoming Qui-Gon's humble servant? TPM

3. What was Jar Jar's hidden underwater city called? TPM

4. What was the name of the military official who marched Jar Jar off to the Boss's Board Room? TPM

5. What was the speediest way to travel from Jar Jar's city to the Naboo capital? TPM

6. What was a bongo? TPM

7. How did Jar Jar describe the Force? TPM

8. What did Anakin tell Jar Jar to do in order to stop the hopping droid in Watto's shop? TPM

9. When Gungans were in trouble, where did they go? TPM

10. What did Captain Tarpals say to Jar Jar as the battle droids entered the Gungans' protective field? TPM

11. When Qui-Gon told Jar Jar "don't do that again" at Anakin's house, what had Jar Jar done? TPM

12. How did Jar Jar hurt his tongue in Anakin's yard in TPM?

13. What did Jar Jar keep saying about his tongue after it had been electrocuted? TPM

14. How did Jar Jar describe the Gungan army to Padmé when they were alone together on Coruscant? TPM

15. What rank did Jar Jar get promoted to on the Naboo battle-field? TPM

16. What was Jar Jar's reaction to being promoted to the top of the Gungan military? TPM

17. What was the name of Jar Jar's exalted Gungan leader? TPM

18. Why did Jar Jar's leader give Jar Jar a military promotion? TPM

19. What was Jar Jar's first command to his troops in the Battle of Naboo? TPM

20. What species was the large, two-legged bird/reptile hybrid that Jar Jar rode in the Battle of Naboo? TPM

21. What happened when Jar Jar got the wires of a battle droid stuck on his foot during the Battle of Naboo? TPM

Jar Jar was conceived of and named by George Lucas's daughter. Jar Jar was loosely based on the character Gunga Din, a childish British Army water boy who manages to save the day.

The Jedi Order

1. Who was the only non-Jedi human to use a lightsaber in any film?
2. What was the name of the group of Jedi leaders known as?
3. What did Luke put over his eyes to test the power of the Force on the Millennium Falcon? ANH
4. Where was Luke when he got his first lightsaber?
5. When the Force allowed Luke to see the future for the first time, what did he see?

6. What did Obi-Wan call Luke's first positive experiences with the Force? ANH

7. Darth Vader told Tarkin that a certain feeling indicated that Obi-Wan was on the Death Star. What was that feeling? ANH

8. After Luke left Tatooine in ROJ, on whom (or what) did he next use his light saber?

9. What was Qui-Gon's last name? TPM

10. Who were the two Jedi knights sent to solve the Naboo crisis? TPM

11. What was the title of the younger of the two Jedi knights dispatched to Naboo? TPM

12. How did the destroyer droids arrive to confront Qui-Gon and Obi-Wan, and what did they use to defend themselves? TPM

13. How did Qui-Gon and Obi-Wan escape the destroyer droids? TPM

14. What agreement ensured that young Anakin would be trained as a Jedi?

15. On which planet is the Jedi Temple?

16. How did Mace Windu describe the role of Jedis in AOC?

17. What line follows "Easy. Jedi business," in AOC?

18. What did the Jedi call the children who were not yet Padawan learners?

George Lucas developed the word "Jedi" from the Japanese phrase *jidai geki*, which means "films about the samurai era."

19. Which Jedi did the Kamino Prime Minister say commissioned the clone army? AOC

20. What's the name of the first clone with whom Obi-Wan communicated in ROS?

21. Where did Obi-Wan tell Anakin that Master Vos had moved his troops? ROS

22. According to Palpatine, why would the Jedi Council accept Palpatine's promotion of Anakin? ROS

23. While in the Jedi Council, whose system did Obi-Wan say they could not afford to lose? ROS

24. When it came to leadership, Obi-Wan said to Anakin the allegiance of the Jedi was with whom? ROS

25. What did Anakin say was the key difference between the Sith and the Jedi? ROS

26. Who was the first person in ROS to say "May the Force be with you"?

27. What reason did Mace Windu give for violating the Jedi code by insisting that Palpatine be killed? ROS

28. Why weren't Yoda or Obi-Wan killed in the purge of the Jedi? ROS

29. Why did Yoda and Obi-Wan want to re-enter the Jedi Temple after the massacre? ROS

30. What was the prophecy of the Chosen One?

31. In which original trilogy film was the prophecy of the Chosen One first mentioned?

32. Was the prophecy of the Chosen One accepted by the Jedi as unquestioned truth?

33. What was the ancent Sith name for the dark side of the Force—one that was used in stories other than the films.

34. What was the opposite of the dark side of the Force officially called?

Lando Calrissian

1. When Leia first heard Han mention Lando, what did she think the name meant? ESB
2. With what three words did Han first describe Lando to Leia?
3. Over what planet was Lando's Cloud City found?
4. What kind of business did Lando run?
5. According to Han, how did Lando come across his Cloud City mine? ESB
6. How many of Lando's aircraft scrambled around the Millennium Falcon as it approached the Cloud City, and what color were they? ESB
7. What did Lando call Han as they meet in ESB for the first time?

Billy Dee Williams first auditioned for the role of Han Solo in ANH.

8. How did Lando describe his role in the Cloud City to Leia when he met her? ESB

9. With what gesture did Lando introduce himself to Leia? ESB

10. What problems of Lando's made Han say that Lando sounded like a businessman? ESB

11. What two major organizations did Lando say his mine was proudly not a member of? ESB

12. What caused Lando to help Darth Vader capture Han and the others on the Cloud City? ESB

13. Darth Vader told Lando that it would be unfortunate if Vader had to do something. What? ESB

14. What did Lando do, wardrobe-wise, in the Cloud City prison as he apologized to Han and said he'd done all he could? ESB

Lando was originally scripted to perish, along with the Millennium Falcon, during the explosion of the second Death Star.

15. With what gesture did we learn that Lando was willing to defy the Empire and help the rebels? ESB

16. What kind of weapon was Lando holding when he was incognito in Jabba's palace? ROJ

17. What was the name of the creature in the sand who almost swallowed Lando in ROJ?

18. As Lando was being pulled down into the pit, what did he yell to Han as Han aimed a blaster at the monster? ROJ

19. What rank did Lando ultimately receive in the Rebel forces? ROJ

20. Lando told Han in ROJ that Lando had been promoted in rank because of a little maneuver in what battle?

21. What did Han say when Lando asked why Han wasn't asked to be leader? ROJ

22. Lando told Han in ROJ that he'd take care of the Millennium Falcon in the raid on the second Death Star, and promised she wouldn't _____.

23. Lando told co-pilot Nien Nunb in ROJ that his friends would have the Death Star's shield generator down in time, or _____.

24. How did Lando determine that the shield was still protecting the Death Star as the attack began in ROJ?

25. Though he was expected to retreat, what was General Calrissian's command for the Rebel fleet attacking the Death Star? ROJ

26. Which were the two colors of squadrons directed by Lando into the Death Star after the shields were down? ROJ

27. Which color squadron was Lando leading against the Death Star in ROJ?

28. While flying inside the Death Star, what did Lando say was "too close"? ROJ

Luke Skywalker

1. What did Darth Vader do the first time Luke saw him?
2. What did Luke do the first time Darth Vader saw him?
3. What was Obi-Wan's first message to Luke as a Force ghost? ANH
4. What did Luke's Uncle Owen do for a living? ANH
5. Why did Uncle Owen want Luke not to enter the academy right away? ANH
6. What had Uncle Owen told Luke that Anakin had done for a living? ANH
7. Where was Luke trying to go in order to avoid having to clean the droids? ANH
8. What did Luke say he needed to get at Tosche Station? ANH
9. How long did Luke tell the stormtroopers at Mos Eisley he had owned C-3PO and R2-D2? ANH
10. What did Luke call the trash compacter while communicating with C-3PO? ANH
11. The last time Luke went to see Uncle Owen and Aunt Beru, what did he find? ANH
12. What did Luke say hitting the target on the Death Star would be as easy as? ANH
13. What canyon on Tatooine did Luke claim the Death Star's trench resembled? ANH
14. What kind of creature attacked Luke at the beginning of ESB?
15. What was Luke's call sign at the beginning of ESB?
16. What did Luke ask his tauntaun just before they were attacked on Hoth? ESB
17. By which leg was Luke dragged into the snow creature's cave? ESB

18. What was Luke's rank on Hoth? ESB
19. What did Luke report the landing of the probe droid to be? ESB
20. What was Luke's call sign in the Rogue Squadron during the Hoth battle in ESB?
21. What was the name of the gunner who flew with Luke in his snowspeeder? ESB
22. As the Battle of Hoth began, Dack told Luke he wasn't ready, he didn't have something. What? ESB
23. What did Luke pull from his crashed snowspeeder just before the Imperial walker destroyed it? ESB
24. What was Luke's first act of using the Force in ESB?
25. Who was the first person Luke saw as he arrived on the Cloud City? ESB
26. What happened on the morning before Mark Hamill filmed the scene with Luke hanging from the bottom of the Cloud City? ESB

27. What did the first line in the opening text of ROJ explain about Luke?

28. According to the opening text in ROJ, what didn't Luke know?

29. How did Luke describe himself in the hologram R2-D2 shows Jabba? ROJ

30. Why did Luke say he seeks an audience with Jabba? ROJ

31. Did Luke enter Jabba's palace in daytime or nighttime? ROJ

32. At what point in what film did Luke use a Force choke similar to Darth Vader's?

33. What choice did Luke give Jabba when Luke said he was taking Captain Solo? ROJ

During the filming of ANH, Mark Hamill burst a blood vessel holding his breath, damaged his wrist jumping onto the Millennium Falcon, and sustained other injuries as well.

34. What two low-tech weapons did Luke use to defeat Jabba's giant monster Rancor?

35. How did Luke get his lightsaber as he walked the plank for Jabba? ROJ

36. What was Luke's last line of dialog on Tatooine?

37. Where did Luke realize that Leia was his sister?

38. Why did Obi-Wan tell Luke to bury his feelings deep down about his father and sister? ROJ

39. What made Luke nervous while awaiting acceptance of the stolen Imperial shuttle's clearance code? ROJ

40. What did Luke say when Vader sensed his presence on the ship?

41. How did Luke address Darth Vader throughout ROJ?

42. What did Luke say was the Emperor's weakness? ROJ

43. What did the Emperor say was Luke's weakness? ROJ

44. As Luke was being brought to the Emperor in ROJ, who got on the elevator with him, and who got off?

45. What, said the Emperor, could Luke witness out the throne room window of the Death Star? ROJ

46. How many actors played Luke onscreen?

In earlier screenplays, Luke was
a girl, a dwarf, a man in his 60's,
or had the last name Starkiller.

The Millennium Falcon

1. Han told Obi-Wan in the cantina that the Millennium Falcon could go precisely how fast? ANH

2. Han boasted the Millennium Falcon accomplished what in 12 parsecs?

3. The Millennium Falcon was docked in which docking bay on Tatooine? ANH

4. How many Imperial ships followed the Millennium Falcon as it blasted off from Tatooine? ANH

5. What piece of technology on the Millennium Falcon did Han use to get the hyperspace coordinates in ANH?

6. What happened when Chewbacca cut the sublight engines on the Millennium Falcon? ANH

7. Where did the Millennium Falcon come out of hyperspace the first time in ANH?

8. What did Han and Chewbacca find when they chased their first TIE fighter in ANH?

9. Why couldn't the Millennium Falcon simply fly away from the Death Star when it first arrived near it? ANH

10. Which docking bay on the Death Star did the Millennium Falcon land on? ANH

11. According to a stormtrooper on the Death Star, what had been jettisoned on the Millennium Falcon? ANH

12. Where were the passengers on the Millennium Falcon hiding when the ship landed on the Death Star? ANH

13. While the Millennium Falcon was on the Death Star, a stormtrooper left his post to go aboard the Falcon. What was his serial number? ANH

14. What WWII-era plane inspired the Millennium Falcon's cockpit?

15. What classification of ship was the Millennium Falcon?

16. What exactly did C-3PO say was broken on the Milennium Falcon's hyperdrive? ESB

17. Which bat-like creatures attached themselves to the Millennium Falcon when it was hiding on the asteroid? ESB

18. Han said that these bat-like creatures in the asteroid would do what to the Millennium Falcon? ESB

19. On what platform did the Falcon land in the Cloud City? ESB

20. Two competing ship designs were developed for George Lucas for the Millennium Falcon. Where was the other design used?

21. How did the Milennium Falcon's pilots locate the Death Star's power generator as they approached in ROJ?

22. What did Han say when he looked at the Millennium Falcon just before leaving for Endor's moon? ROJ
23. Did Han see the Falcon again?
24. In what other Harrison Ford film did the Millennium Falcon make an unbilled appearance?

The Millennium Falcon actually made a special guest appearance in ROS. Look for it landing on the lowest level of the circular landing area in Coruscant, just before Obi-Wan and Anakin discussed which of them was the hero for saving Palpatine.

Obi-Wan Kenobi

1. Chronologically, what was Obi-Wan's first line on film?
2. Kenobi was said to live beyond what geographical marker on Tatooine? ANH
3. What did Uncle Owen call Obi-Wan when Luke first mentioned Obi-Wan to him? ANH
4. How did Obi-Wan save an unconscious Luke from the Sand People? ANH

**Ewan McGregor requested a loop
of video showing every scene with Sir Alec
Guinness, in order to better create
the younger Obi-Wan.**

5. What military rank did Leia attribute to Obi-Wan as a result of the Clone Wars? ANH

6. As the Millennium Falcon was being dragged into the Death Star, Obi-Wan said they couldn't win, but suggested what advice to Han? ANH

7. Finish this sentence from ANH: "Who's the more foolish _____?"

8. What were the last two lines of dialog Obi-Wan said to Luke on the Death Star? ANH

9. What did Obi-Wan do to help the Rebels while on the Death Star? ANH

10. What did Obi-Wan tell Darth Vader would happen if Vader struck him down? ANH

11. What action of Obi-Wan's caused his death? ANH

12. Why did Obi-Wan allow himself to be killed? ANH

13. In ROJ, how did Obi-Wan justify his previous explanation in ANH that Darth Vader killed Luke's father?

14. According to Obi-Wan, what do the truths we cling to depend on? ROJ

15. Obi-Wan told Luke in ROJ that he thought he could train Anakin as a Jedi just as well as Yoda, but _____.

16. In ROJ, how did Obi-Wan describe what's left of his old friend Anakin to Luke on Dagobah?

17. When did Obi-Wan tell Luke that the Emperor had already won?

18. How old was Obi-Wan supposed to be in ANH, and how old was Sir Alec Guinness during filming?

19. Obi-Wan greeted R2-D2 (in ANH) and General Grievous (in ROS) for the first time with what two words?

20. What phrase did Obi-Wan use to describe Anakin just prior to their first meeting?

21. What did Obi-Wan say to Anakin as they met for the first time?

22. With what did Obi-Wan kill Darth Maul? TPM

23. With what words from Yoda did Obi-Wan pass from Padawan to Jedi?

24. Where did Obi-Wan return from when he was assigned to protect Padmé on Coruscant? AOC

25. Obi-Wan told Anakin in an elevator that he hasn't seen Anakin this tense since they fell into a nest of what? AOC

26. What happened when Obi-Wan and Anakin fell into that nest? AOC

27. What exactly did Obi-Wan think about politicians? AOC

28. What did the seedy salesman in the Coruscant bar try to sell to Obi-Wan? AOC

29. What was Obi-Wan's advice to the seedy salesman in the Coruscant bar? AOC

30. How did Obi-Wan defeat the guided missile that Jango Fett used against Obi-Wan's ship? AOC

Before Alec Guinness was cast in ANH, Peter Cushing (who played Tarkin) was considered for the part.

31. While approaching the massive ringed planet Geonosis, what did Obi-Wan discover an unusual concentration of? AOC

32. What aspect of a Jedi's responsibilities did Obi-Wan say several times in the prequel trilogy he disliked?

33. What was the first thing Obi-Wan did when he crash landed on General Dooku's command ship? ROS

34. What was Obi-Wan's comment immediately after the disintegrating command ship Anakin was piloting broke in half? ROS

35. After Anakin said he'd saved Obi-Wan for the tenth time, what was his master's reply? ROS

36. What did Obi-Wan ask Anakin to do to secretly help the Jedi Council? ROS

37. According to Obi-Wan, not even these people survived the Jedi Temple massacre. Who? ROS

38. How did Obi-Wan find Darth Vader for their fiery showdown on Mustafar? ROS

39. What was Obi-Wan's reply when a crippled Darth Vader yelled, "I hate you!" in ROS?

40. Which characters were waiting for Obi-Wan on Padmé's ship when he returned from his duel with Darth Vader? ROS

41. What special training did Yoda have Obi-Wan undertake while watching over the baby Luke on Tatooine? ROS

Original Trilogy Characters

1. What was the first line of dialog in ANH, and who said it?

2. Who was the last character to speak in ANH?

3. Who was Luke's best friend on Tatooine (whose part was mostly cut from ANH), who died on the final assault of the Death Star?

4. What happened to the Jawas who sold the droids to Luke? ANH

5. Which Rebel official led the planning meeting to explain the attack of the Death Star? ANH

6. Who approached Luke's landspeeder once it was parked in Mos Eisley? ANH

7. Who said that the droids weren't welcome in the cantina? ANH

8. What did Obi-Wan and Luke do with the bodies of the dead Jawas on Tatooine? ANH

9. How many Tusken Raiders raided the unconscious Luke's land-speeder? ANH

10. Biggs told Red Leader that Luke was what kind of pilot? ANH

11. What was Red Leader's reply when Wedge saw the Death Star and said, "Look at the size of that thing!"? ANH

12. Who was the first character seen in ESB?

13. What was the name of the two-legged animal Luke rode on Hoth? ESB

14. General Rieekan said no Rebel ships could leave the Hoth sys-tem until what happened? ESB

The cantina band was not originally planned: it was a last-minute addition. For budgetary reasons, most of the cantina characters wore masks rather than special makeup.

15. In ESB, after they said farewell on Hoth, where would Luke and Han next meet?

16. How many little red circles were seen on General Rieekan's uniform as the Rebels were evacuating Hoth? ESB

17. What was the name of Lando's bald assistant with the original wraparound Bluetooth headset? ESB

18. Which short aliens operated the Cloud City's carbon-freezing and trash operations? ESB

19. Who was Rogue Three during the Battle of Hoth? ESB

20. What, according to the subtitles on the ROJ DVD, was the language spoken by the bounty hunter who came to sell Chewbacca to Jabba?

21. What was the name of the bounty hunter who came to Jabba's Palace (as opposed to the person's secret identity)? ROJ

22. What was the explosive device the bounty hunter held when negotiating with Jabba for Chewbacca? ROJ

23. What was the toad-like creature doing in the sand outside Jabba's palace just after Chewbacca was put in a jail cell? ROJ

24. As the bounty hunter took a frozen Han off the wall, you can see a gloved hand close up. What was on the back of the glove? ROJ

25. Who was hiding in the bounty hunter's costume? ROJ

26. How many claws did the monster under Jabba's pit have on each hand-like appendage? ROJ

27. Exactly how was the Sarlacc supposed to kill Luke and the others in ROJ?

28. How did Boba Fett die?

29. What was the name of the woman led the Rebel Alliance in ROJ?

30. What was the name and species of the salmon-colored, fish-faced Rebel admiral in charge of the assault on the Death Star? ROJ

31. Who was the field general in charge of the fighter attack on the Death Star? ROJ

32. What was the name of the general who told the Rebel leaders that the rebels had stolen an Imperial ship, and what kind of ship was it? ROJ

33. Who was the general in charge of the ground troops on Endor? ROJ

34. When was the first time the word "Ewok" was mentioned onscreen in ROJ?

35. Where was the only place that the word Ewok was used in the six films?

36. What happened after Leia gave Wicket, the first Ewok, something to eat? ROJ

37. How did Luke, Han, Chewbacca, and the droids escape the Ewok's net trap? ROJ

38. What caused the Ewoks to begin chanting and bowing? ROJ

39. What plans did the Ewoks have for the recently captured (and bound) Han? ROJ

40. Who played Lando's co-pilot, Nien Nunb, in ROJ, and what actual Earth language did he speak?

41. What was General Ackbar's call sign in ROJ?

42. What did R2-D2 and Paploo, the speeder-stealing Ewok, have in common? ROJ

43. Which pilot got the honor of aiming the death blows at the second Death Star? ROJ

44. What acted as a sort of kettle drum set for Ewok musicians at the end of ROJ?

45. Which major characters got a nonfatal arm wound in ROJ?

Padmé Amidala

1. What film series did Natalie Portman believe she'd been asked to read for when first approached?

2. What royal name had Padmé assumed when she became queen of Naboo?

3. What age was Padmé when she was queen of Naboo in TPM?

4. What was the location of the red makeup that queens in Naboo wore when serving their official function?

5. What color is Padmé's thumbnail in TPM?

6. What was the name of the head of the Royal Naboo Security Forces, who accompanied Queen Amidala and her retinue off Naboo? TPM

7. Where did Padmé tell Anakin their ship was waiting on Tatooine? TPM

8. Why did Obi-Wan forbid Padmé to reply to the distress hologram from Naboo? TPM

9. Why was the Trade Federation actively seeking Padmé? TPM

10. What is the name of the Queen who succeeded Padmé as leader of the Naboo?

11. What was the name of Padmé's white-haired male adviser, the governor of Naboo?

12. What diplomatic masterstroke of Padmé's ultimately allowed her to regain control of her planet from the Trade Federation? TPM

Whenever Natalie Portman portrayed Padmé, her natural voice was heard. As Queen Amidala, her voice was altered digitally.

13. What was the name of Padmé's capital city?

14. How did Padmé, Panaka, and their invasion force reach the upper floor of their palace as they re-took it? TPM

15. What was Padmé's next career move after abdicating the position of queen of Naboo?

16. What was the name of Padmé's decoy who died at the beginning of AOC?

17. What was the name of Padmé's security guard in the first scene of AOC, and what was the purpose of that thing on his eye?

18. What was the name of the poisonous creatures that were sent to kill Padmé in her bedroom in AOC?

19. According to Padmé, what would happen if the Separatists were offered violence? AOC

20. What was the name of Padmé's second decoy handmaiden in AOC?

21. What did Padmé say to Anakin immediately after their first kiss?

22. Who was Padmé's first love, and what happened to him?

23. What happened in AOC in the scene immediately after Anakin fell off a massive animal (called a Shaak) and Padmé and Anakin rolled around in the grass?

24. What did Padmé do after she learned that Anakin had slaughtered all of the Tusken Raiders, even the women and children? AOC

25. What injury did Padmé receive in the arena on Geonosis? AOC

26. What was notable about Padmé's hair in her first scene in ROS?

27. What did Padmé say would happen to Anakin and herself if they were known to be married and expecting? ROS

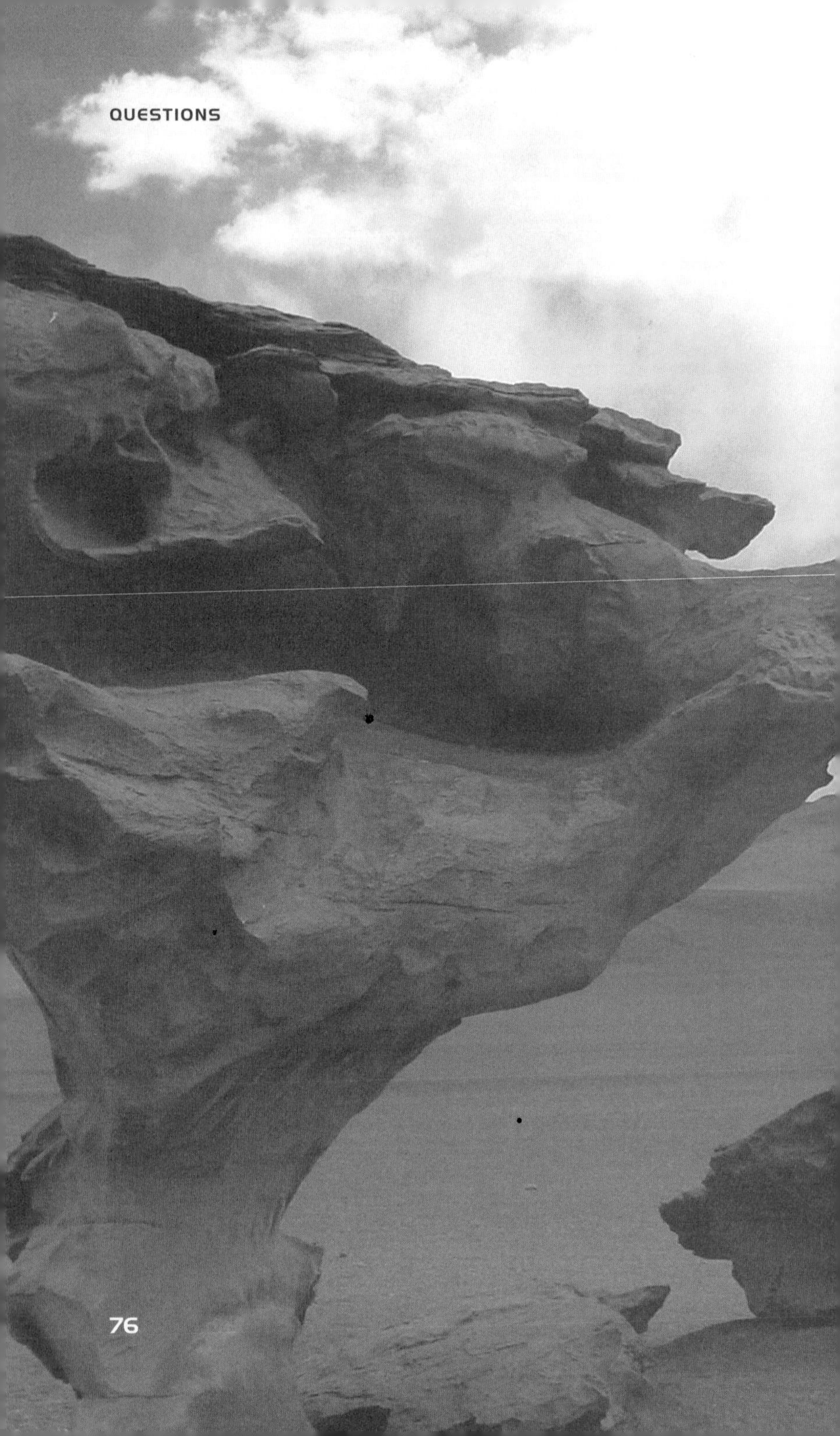

28. What did Padmé ask Anakin to tell the chancellor to do, now that Anakin was closest to the chancellor? ROS

29. Who told Padmé to save her energy? ROS

30. What did the medical droid say Padmé had lost during her childbirth scene? ROS

31. Who was born first, Luke or Leia?

32. What was in Padmé's hand during her last scene in ROS, and what else was she doing in that scene?

33. How did Padmé die, according to Darth Sidious?

34. Did Padmé meet the foster parents for each of her children?

35. Can it be argued that Padmé is responsible for the destruction of the Jedi and the rise of the Empire?

Padmé means lotus flower in Sanskrit, and Nabirye (her last name) means mother of twins in Egyptian.

The Planets

1. Where and when did the Star Wars films take place?
2. What was the first planet we saw in ANH, and the last planet we saw in ROS?
3. What planet was supposed to be where instead an asteroid field was found? ANH
4. Where exactly was the Rebel base located in ANH?
5. On which planet did Princess Leia tell Tarkin the Rebel base was located? ANH
6. What was the name of the ice planet in ESB?
7. According to Han, there wasn't enough life on Hoth to do what? ESB
8. Approaching Dagobah for the first time, Luke found no cities or technology, but what did his scanner find? ESB
9. What did Luke say against Dagobah that offended Yoda? ESB
10. When the Millennium Falcon was hidden on the back of an Imperial Star Destroyer, in what star system were they located? ESB
11. To which system did Luke and R2-D2 fly directly after leaving Tatooine for the last time? ROJ
12. Which celestial body was the second Death Star orbiting? ROJ
13. Darth Vader had received reports of the Rebel fleet massing near where? ROJ

The Galaxy has never been given a name, such as the Milky Way. It is always just the Galaxy.

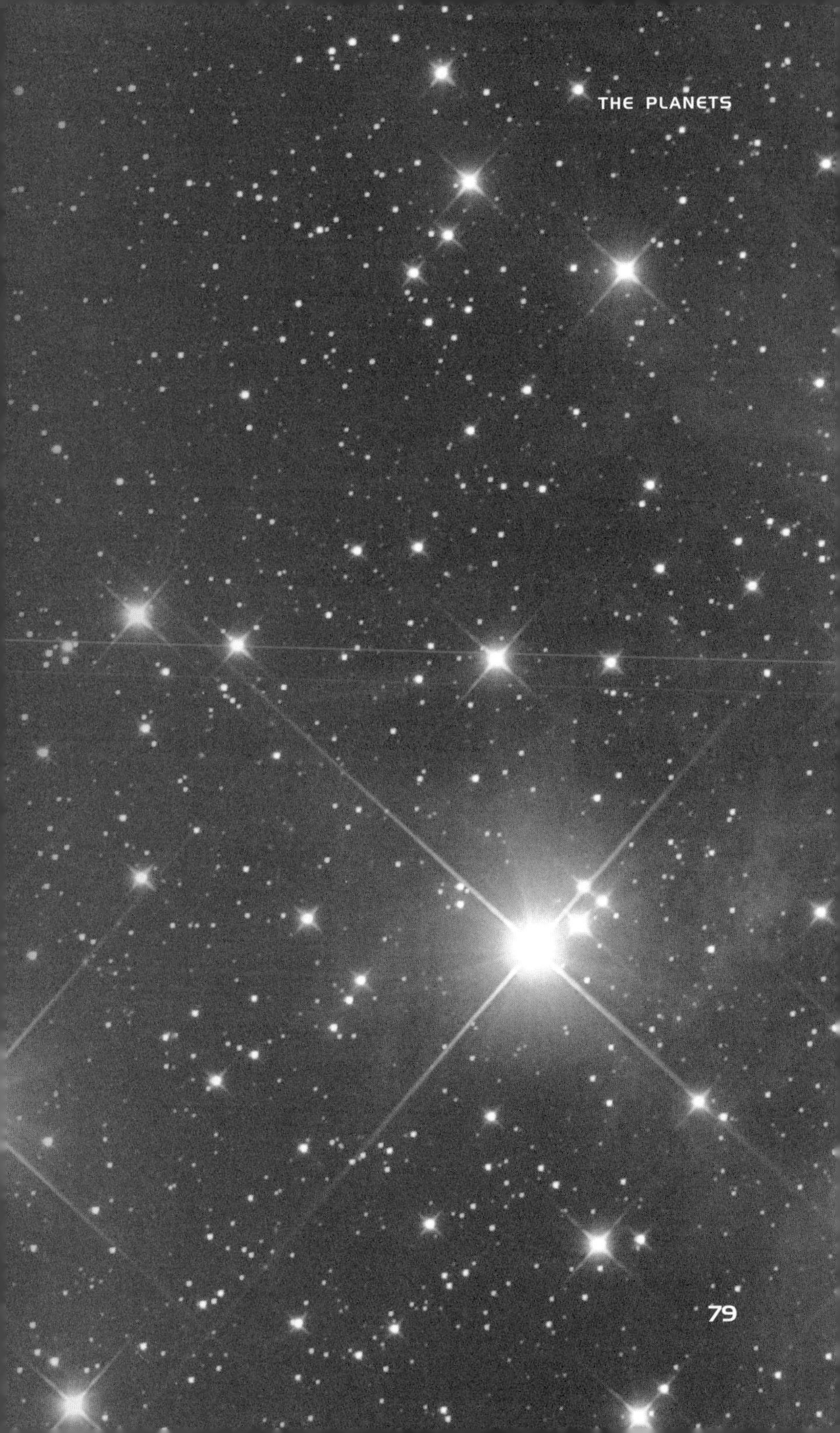

14. Where exactly did the Emperor tell Darth Vader to wait for Luke in ROJ?

15. On which planet was the destruction of the Death Star celebrated first? ROJ

16. What planet did the Jedi knights attempt to take Queen Amidala and her party to when they were sidetracked? TPM

17. What was notable about the planet Coruscant, as it was described? TPM

18. What planet was the Emperor from?

19. What was the name of the nearest landmark (so to speak) to the Kamino system? AOC

20. What appeared to be the primary export of the planet Geonosis? AOC

21. What was the name of the Wookiee's planet, and which Jedi Master took responsibility for protecting it? ROS

22. Where, said Palpatine to Anakin at the theater, was General Grievous hiding? ROS

23. To what star system did Anakin go to slaughter Nute Gunray and the other Separatists? ROS

24. Besides being cool to look at, what was the official purpose of the flaming volcanic location on Mustafar?

25. At the very end of the Special Edition of ROJ, there were mass celebrations in four distant but familiar locations. What were they, and in what order?

According to Steven Spielberg,
the movie character E.T. was supposed
to have been from the same galaxy,
but not from a long time ago.

Prequel Trilogy Characters

1. What was the name of the junk dealer on Tatooine who owned Anakin? TPM

2. Which of the Tatooine junk dealer's large teeth is clearly broken? TPM

3. What colors were seen on Watto's chance cube? TPM

4. What was the name and the race of the creature who raced Anakin in TPM?

5. Which head of the two-headed announcer at the pod race spoke Huttese? TPM

6. Who was the two-time pod race winner who was announced just prior to Sebulba at the start of the pod race? TPM

7. Who was announced as "hoping for a big win today" at the pod races? TPM

8. Who called whom "bantha poodoo"? TPM

9. Whose power coupling went straight into the air in the pod race? TPM

10. What did Sebulba say when he lost the pod race? TPM

11. Who else was nominated to run as supreme chancellor against Senator Palpatine? TPM

12. Who got the last word at the end of TPM?

13. The characters in AOC are how many years older than they were in TPM?

14. What was the name of the four-armed owner of the Coruscant diner? AOC

15. Where did the Coruscant diner owner in AOC last see a poisonous dart like the one Obi-Wan showed him, and to what group did it belong?

Every single clone trooper in ROS was created using computer graphics.

16. What did the diner owner on Coruscant say were two traits that help with getting on the good side of the Kaminoans? AOC

17. What was the name of the prime minister of Kamino? AOC

18. Why were clones immensely superior to droids, according to the Kamino prime minister? AOC

19. Who was the original host to the clone army? AOC

20. What was Shmi doing when she was abducted? AOC

21. What was the name of the man who married Shmi? AOC

22. How did Padmé, Obi-Wan, and Anakin each escape their chains in the arena on Geonosis? AOC

23. How many commando units of clones were reported waiting for Mace Windu's orders at the start of the Clone Wars? AOC

24. What was the last line of dialog in AOC?

25. What was the first word in the text crawl at the beginning of ROS?

26. In what film was Bail Organa's first line of dialog, and what was his role at the time?

27. What was the name of the green-armored clone commander on Kashyyyk? ROS

28. Who killed Mace Windu?

29. What was the name of the Clone Commander who gave Obi-Wan back his lightsaber? ROS

30. In ROS, who told Bail Organa, "Hopefully we'll be able to intercept a few Jedi before they walk into this catastrophe," and what was his claim to fame in ANH?

31. What were Shmi's last words? AOC

32. What were Darth Vader's last words before his suit was fastened to him?

Darth Maul was originally supposed to be played by Benicio del Toro, who left after most of the character's lines were cut.

Princess Leia

1. What was Leia doing the first time her sweet and memorable musical theme was heard? ANH
2. What was the official name and type of Princess Leia's ship? ANH
3. When did Luke first see Leia? ANH
4. What was Princess Leia's first comment to Darth Vader?

Leia was named for Leah Adler, the mother of Lucas's good friend Steven Spielberg.

5. What evidence did Darth Vader confront Princess Leia with proved to him that she was a spy? ANH

6. In Leia's transmission to Obi-Wan, she asked him to bring the information in R2-D2 to whom? ANH

7. In which detention block on the Death Star did R2-D2 say Princess Leia was being held? ANH

8. What was Leia's first comment to Luke? ANH

9. What was Princess Leia's adoptive father's full name?

10. What was Leia's first comment to Han? ANH

11. What was Han's first comment to Leia? ANH

12. What did Leia tell Han just before jumping into the Death Star's trash compactor? ANH

13. What did Leia say to Han after he used his blaster inside the trash compactor? ANH
14. Who gave Leia the medals that she put on Luke and Han at the end of ANH?
15. How old was Carrie Fisher during the principal shooting of ANH?
16. Who would Leia "just as soon kiss" as Han in the beginning of ESB?
17. What kind of brain did Leia accuse Han of having in the Hoth medical center? ESB
18. What long, four-part insult did Leia give Han in the medical center on Hoth? ESB
19. What caused Leia to evacuate Hoth with Han rather than on her transport? ESB
20. What did Leia say Han was usually acting like-just before their first kiss-and what was his reply?

21. What was Leia doing just before Han kissed her for the first time? ESB

22. What did Leia yell to Luke when she saw him on the Cloud City? ESB

23. Who was the familiar guard who dragged Leia toward Jabba for the first time in his palace? ROJ

24. What effort broke the chain that bound Leia to Jabba? ROJ

25. While piloting the speeder bike, what did Leia do to stop the stormtroopers from communicating with command? ROJ

26. What was Leia's first comment to the Ewok who awakened her on the forest floor? ROJ

27. What did Leia remember about her real mother? ROJ

28. What was Leia's full name at birth?

29. How did Leia describe the Force just before finding out the truth of her relationship to Luke and Darth Vader? ROJ

30. What were Luke and Leia standing on when he told her that she was his sister? ROJ

31. After Leia had been hit in the arm by a blaster, what caused Han to tell her, "I love you"? ROJ

32. How many actresses played Leia onscreen?

33. How unfair was it that Leia got to grow up as a princess on a lush planet while her twin brother had to live like an unhappy lizard on a desert rock? ROS

The youngest princess of Norway, Leah Isadora, born in 2005, was named for Princess Leia (and indirectly for Steven Spielberg's mother!)

Qui-Gon Jinn

1. How did Qui-Gon pronounce his name? TPM

2. What was Qui-Gon's first line in TPM?

3. What was Qui-Gon's first line of dialog in AOC?

4. How did Qui-Gon respond when Obi-Wan said, "I have a bad feeling about this"? TPM

5. What separated Qui-Gon and Darth Maul from Obi-Wan in their three-way lightsaber duel in TPM?

6. How much money did Qui-Gon have to buy the hyperdrive generator? TPM

7. Why couldn't Qui-Gon convince Watto to take the money? TPM

8. What words did Qui-Gon use to describe Anakin to Obi-Wan for the first time? TPM

9. What did Qui-Gon test Anakin's blood for? TPM

10. How did Qui-Gon raise the money he needed for the parts to the Naboo ship? TPM

11. What secret knowledge did Qui-Gon discover about the Force in TPM that was a surprise to Darth Vader in ANH?

12. Qui-Gon said to Obi-Wan on the Trade Federation ship that he sensed an unusual amount of what? TPM

13. What gas did Qui-Gon recognize entering the room on the Trade Federation ship in TPM?

14. What did Anakin call the fruit that Qui-Gon got from Jira, the peddler woman on Tatooine? TPM

15. Qui-Gon told young Anakin that to race pods, the boy must have what? TPM

16. How did Qui-Gon keep Jar Jar from slurping up extra fruit with his tongue? TPM

17. What did Qui-Gon say would be his entry fee in the pod race? TPM

18. At the pod race, Qui-Gon promised Watto his winnings at what time of day? TPM

19. When Qui-Gon managed to get Watto to bet for Anakin's freedom, what were the stakes? TPM

20. How did Qui-Gon win against Watto's betting cube? TPM

21. How did Qui-Gon's first battle with Darth Maul end? TPM

22. Where did Qui-Gon tell Anakin to stay at the beginning of the Battle of Naboo? TPM

23. What did Qui-Gon do while the force field separated him from Darth Maul in their final battle? TPM

24. What blow did Qui-Gon receive from Darth Maul just prior to his fatal injury? TPM

25. What was the relationship between Qui-Gon and Count Dooku?

George Lucas originally intended to shoot a scene in ROS showing a transparent Qui-Gon introducing the idea of Force ghosts to Yoda, but Liam Neeson was busy shooting *Batman Begins* at the time.

When R2-D2 was moving smoothly,
it was a remote control unit. When it stood
still or seemed to hop, Kenny Baker
was inside.

R2-D2

1. Where did R2-D2 first meet C-3PO?

2. Chronologically, what was the first heroic effort of R2-D2? TPM

3. R2-D2 and C-3PO fell under what classification in the Star Wars universe?

4. Who owned R2-D2 and C-3PO just before they found themselves on Tatooine? ANH

5. What malfunctioned on the red R2 unit that Uncle Owen originally bought, paving the way for Luke to get R2-D2? ANH

6. What did Luke find on R2-D2 that made him believe the droids had seen a lot of action? ANH

7. What did R2-D2 say kept him from showing Luke the entire message from Princess Leia? ANH

8. While Obi-Wan was using Jedi mind tricks on the Imperial stormtroopers at Mos Eisley, what was R2-D2 doing in Luke's speeder? ANH

9. What was hidden inside R2-D2? ANH

10. What did Luke ask R2-D2 to repair on his ship during the assault on the Death Star? ANH

11. C-3PO offered to donate what general items to help fix the fried R2-D2 at the end of ANH?

12. What kind of heater did C-3PO say R2-D2 turned on in Leia's chamber? ESB

13. What did R2-D2 compute to be the chances of Luke or Han's survival out in the cold of Hoth? ESB

14. What gift did R2-D2 announce, via C-3PO, he had brought to Jabba? ROJ

15. Where did R2-D2 get assigned to work for Jabba? ROJ

16. What did R2-D2 do in his job for Jabba? ROJ

17. What stopped R2-D2 from opening the door on the command bunker in ROJ?

18. What mechanical ability did R2-D2 reveal just before saving Padmé on the assembly line in AOC?

19. What was the strategy for an R2 unit to remove an unwanted buzz droid from a flying spacecraft? AOC

20. Where on Dooku's command ship did R2-D2 locate the chancellor's signal? AOC

21. How did R2-D2 disable two super battle droids in the hangar bay of Dooku's command ship? AOC

22. How many of the six films showed R2-D2 and C-3PO in the closing shot?

23. What happened after R2-D2 zapped a super battle droid in hallway 328 of the damaged Trade Federation cruiser in ROS?

24. In which films did R2-D2 save at least one life?

Kenny Baker's R2-D2 costume allowed the diminutive actor to work the lights and appendages himself.

The Rebel Alliance

1. Who was the captain of Princess Leia's ship at the beginning of ANH?
2. What were the two color codes for the Rebel attack squads at the end of ANH?
3. Who briefed the pilots on how to attack the Death Star? ANH
4. Why did the mechanic at the Rebel base on Yavin offer to provide Luke with a different R2 unit than R2-D2? ANH
5. Which two Rebel fighters got killed providing cover to Gold Leader while attacking the Death Star? ANH
6. Who was Red Three during the Death Star assault? ANH
7. What word of advice did Biggs give when Porkins's X-Wing fighter was hit? ANH
8. How many guns did Gold Five think were shooting at the Rebels from the Death Star? ANH
9. Who was the last Rebel to die attacking the Death Star in ANH?
10. What was Biggs Darklighter's last word? ANH
11. As Rebel fighters took off to destroy the Death Star, what was the announced estimated time until the Death Star would be in firing range of the Rebel base? ANH
12. What were pilot Porkins' last words? ANH
13. According to the opening text in ESB, who was leading a group of freedom fighters?

In footage cut from ROS (but included among the deleted scenes on the DVD), Padmé is seen meeting with Bail Organa and others to begin what would become the Rebel Alliance.

14. What was Han's call sign on Hoth? ESB

15. Who was commander of the Rebel base on Hoth? ESB

16. Who on Hoth said his snowspeeder had a problem with the fire control? ESB

17. What was Rebel Officer Derlin's rank? ESB

18. Where did General Rieekan first say the probe droid was located on the Hoth surface? ESB

19. During the attack on the second Death Star, how many X-Wing ships were destroyed? ROJ

20. During the Hoth battle, who was Rogue Leader? ESB

21. What was the code name for the Rebel's base on Hoth? ESB

22. What did Rieekan agree with Han was "not an easy thing to live with"? ESB

23. The deck officer said Han's tauntaun would freeze before reaching what? ESB

24. What was the call sign of the pilot who rescued Han and Luke from Hoth's frigid exterior? ESB

25. While Luke was relaxing after Leia's unsisterlike kiss on Hoth, a voice on the intercom made what request? ESB

26. To which station did General Rieekan scramble Rogues 10 and 11? ESB

27. What did the exploding probe droid on Hoth represent to the Rebels? ESB

28. As the Empire approached Hoth, what did General Rieekan learn was coming out of hyperspace in Sector 4? ESB

29. How many Rebel fighter ships were initially planned to accompany each heavy transport off Hoth? ESB

30. What's the name of the major weapon the Rebels used to protect evacuating transport ships from Hoth? ESB

31. What attack pattern did Luke call out to Dack on Hoth? ESB

32. Since the armor on the Imperial walkers was too strong for blasters, what did Luke tell Rogue Group to use? ESB

33. What did Dack do instead of following Luke's command to fire the tow cable at the Imperial walker? ESB

34. Who flew the ship that bound and tripped the Imperial walker with a tow rope on Hoth? ESB

35. According to a Rebel leader, who had brought the data on the new Death Star to the Rebels? ROJ

36. What key facts did the leader of the Rebel Alliance say they'd learned from the second Death Star plans? ROJ

37. What needed to happen first if the Rebels were to try an attack on the second Death Star? ROJ

38. How did the Rebels expect the stolen shuttle would fool the Empire into letting it land? ROJ

39. What would the Rebels attempt to knock out on the second Death Star in order to destroy it? ROJ

40. What were the human Rebels wearing on Endor, but not the droids? ROJ

41. How did Paploo, the Ewok, create a distraction at the control bunker of the shield generator? ROJ

42. How did the Rebels actually come to learn about the location of the shield generator? ROJ

43. What new color fighter squadrons debuted for the Rebels in ROJ?

44. Where did Admiral Ackbar tell Green Group to stick close to? ROJ

45. What did Admiral Ackbar tell the Rebel fleet to concentrate on, in order to give Lando and his attack crew more time? ROJ

46. Which Rebel pilot (beside Luke) made it through all three original trilogy battles alive?

47. How many Rebel fighters accompanied the Millenium Falcon into the second Death Star? ROJ

The Ships

1. How many engines were visible on Princess Leia's ship in the opening of ANH?

2. What did Darth Vader plan to do with Princess Leia's captured ship? ANH

3. How many Rebel ships did Imperial officials say were attacking the Death Star? ANH

4. What disabled Darth Vader's fighter during the attack on the Death Star? ANH

5. How many Imperial TIE fighters were first seen approaching the Rebel ships in their first wave of defending the Death Star? ANH

6. Why was Darth Vader's TIE fighter different from all other TIE fighters?

7. What command told the X-Wing pilots to separate the wings on their ships? ANH

8. Which type of ships, and how many, were the last to escape the Death Star's explosion? ANH

9. How many TIE fighters followed the Millennium Falcon into the asteroid field? ESB

An Imperial-Class Star Destroyer was one mile long. A Star Destroyer appears in every *Star Wars* film except TPM.

10. How many Star Destroyers can be seen during the first scene of ROJ?

11. How many engines were there on an Imperial shuttle? ROJ

12. Which spacecraft was the first one seen in ROJ?

13. Whose small ship was the first one seen in ROJ?

14. What did the shuttle captain announce was the call sign of Darth Vader's ship, and what type of ship was it? ROJ

15. What vehicle did Luke use to escape the second Death Star? ROJ

16. What was the name of the stolen Imperial shuttle that Han piloted toward Endor? ROJ

17. Whose ship took the lead for the Rebel fleet against the Empire in space? ROJ

18. What kind of Rebel frigate did the Imperial Fleet attack? ROJ

19. During the Rebel fleet's assault, Lando noticed that only the fighters were attacking. Which category of ship appeared to be waiting? ROJ

20. Whose ship left the exploding second Death Star last-Wedge's, Lando's, or Luke's? ROJ

21. At what point did we see Padmé's ship in hologram form? TPM

22. How many rocket thrusters were on the space cruiser which brought the Jedi knights to Naboo? TPM

23. What malfunction required the escaping Naboo spacecraft to land on Tatooine? TPM

More than 100 different types of ship were designed or developed for the *Star Wars* universe.

24. What kind of ship did Qui-Gon say he needed parts for, and where was his parts list? TPM

25. What was the sound effect given to Padmé's ship as it began its descent onto Coruscant at the beginning of AOC?

26. What was notable about the three ships seen immediately after the opening text of AOC?

27. What command from General Grievous caused the plummeting Trade Federation cruiser to level out? ROS

28. What kind of ships arrived to help save the crashing Trade Federation cruiser piloted by Anakin in ROS?

29. What was the purpose of Obi-Wan's transport hyperspace ring, the docking station for his small Eta-2 Jedi starfighter in the prequel trilogy?

30. Whose ship did Obi-Wan use to escape Utapau? ROS

31. What was the category of ship that Obi-Wan crashed onto in ROS and whose was it?

32. What type of ship did Padmé fly to Mustafar to find Anakin? ROS

33. How many rocket thrusters were on the back of the cruiser when Yoda, Obi-Wan, and Bail Organa flew back to Coruscant at the end of ROS?

34. In the scene where Obi-Wan and Yoda discussed the Jedi purge with Bail Organa, what was notable about the corridor of the ship they were in? ROS

Special Effects

1. What was the very first special effects shot ever produced by Industrial Light & Magic? ANH

2. What did the actors hold while filming the lightsaber duel scenes?

3. What was the low-budget solution for making Luke's speeder appear to be flying in ANH?

4. What explosive effect was used on the final TIE fighter in the space battle after the Millennium Falcon left the Death Star? ANH

5. What provided the engine sound of the Star Destroyer? ANH

6. Which old photographic technology was used to make ANH look as good as it did?

7. What is the name of George Lucas's proprietary audio technology company?

8. Compared to the lethal blasts, what was visually different about the stun blast that the Imperial stormtroopers fired on Leia at the beginning of ANH?

9. How were the sounds of the large and small lasers produced?

10. When was Darth Vader's theme music, "The Imperial March," heard playing on a harp?

11. What common nautical device was used for the effect of Darth Vader's heavy breathing?

12. What animal's scream was combined with what automotive activity to create the sound of the Empire's small TIE fighters in action?

In the first battle sequence in ROS, a Clone Star Destroyer is hit by a flying kitchen sink masquerading as space debris.

13. Most of the attendees at the award ceremony at the close of ANH could best be described as what?

14. In each of the original trilogy films, a different percentage of the exterior of the Millennium Falcon was built. Match the percentage to the film: 25%, 50%, 100%

15. What was the low-tech effect that was used when Luke retrieved his lightsaber from the snow? ESB

16. In ESB, what edible item was used as an asteroid?

17. What famous building on a famous California island provided the sound of Darth Vader's shuttle door opening in ESB?

18. How many R2-D2s were used in ESB?

19. What produced the sound of R2-D2 moving smoothly along?

20. What melted under the heat of the lighting in ESB?

21. Who provided the voice of the droid in Jabba's slave yard in ROJ?

22. Which common species of animal provided the voice over for Jabba's monstrous Rancor? ROJ

23. How did sound engineer Ben Burtt produce the sound of Jabba moving?

24. What color did the carbonite turn while Han was getting freed from it? ROJ

25. How were the forest chase sequences in ROJ shot without disturbing the natural wilderness?

George Lucas's first computer development group was sold to Steve Jobs in 1988. He renamed it Pixar.

ANH had 350 visual effects shots.
ROS had over 2,200.

26. What very normal, very earthly object masqueraded as an
Empire ship just after Lando said, "pressure's steady" during
the attack on the Death Star in in ROJ?

27. What appeared briefly on Vader's mask as he watched the
Emperor plummet down the deep shaft? ROJ

28. After the Emperor fell down the shaft, what came back up? ROJ

29. What was notable about the sound effect choice for the
wounded Darth Vader's labored breathing at the end of ROJ?

30. AOC was the first American film to accomplish what technological feat?

31. What was heard on the AOC soundtrack immediately after
Jango Fett's assault weapons detonate?

32. How did 78-year-old Christopher Lee face all the Jedi acrobat-
ics required of Dooku in his double-duel with Obi-Wan and
Anakin? AOC

33. Which NFL team's fans provided the crowd noises for the pod
race in TPM?

34. From a touch-typist's point of view, what's interesting about
the words Star wars?

On ANH's first day of shooting on location, Tunisia experienced its first major rain in about fifty years.

Tatooine

1. If there is a bright center to the universe, then Tatooine is

   _____.

2. How many of the films had scenes on Tatooine?

3. Where in the Galaxy was Tatooine, as described in TPM?

4. What Tatooine native was seen next to C-3PO as he waved to the Jawas' transport for rescue? ANH

5. What beast did the Sand People ride? ANH

6. Where on Tatooine was Luke planning to go to have R2-D2's memory erased? ANH

7. What languages did Luke's uncle want C-3P0 to speak? ANH

8. Where did Luke's uncle want the droids working in the morning? ANH

9. What was another name for the Sand People of Tatooine? ANH

10. In ANH, how many banthas appeared in Luke's macro-binoculars?

These places all represented Tatooine on screen: Djerba, Matmata,Tozeur, Medenine, Ksar Hadada, the Chott El-Djerid, and La Grande Dune (all in Africa); Death Valley and the sand dunes of Yuma in Arizona (in the USA).

11. The deformed fellow who attacked Luke in the cantina was condemned in how many places? ANH

12. Luke couldn't get the full asking price for his landspeeder ever since what new model came out, and what was Luke's model? ANH

13. Where were the Jundland Wastes, and what did Obi-Wan say about them? ANH

14. In which region of Tatooine did Jabba sentence Luke and the others to be killed? ROJ

15. What was the name of the pit in which the Sarlacc lived? ROJ

16. How long would it take the Sarlacc to digest someone? ROJ

17. What reasons did Qui-Gon and Obi-Wan give in deciding Tatooine would be a safe place to repair and refuel the ship? TPM

18. What happened to slaves on Tatooine who attempted to escape? TPM

19. What was the name of the town on Tatooine where Qui-Gon discovered Anakin? TPM

20. About how close to home was Shmi when the Tusken Raiders captured her? AOC

21. Who eventually pointed Anakin in the direction of his mother's abductors? AOC

The Technology

1. What technology did the Jawas use to lift R2-D2 up into their transport? ANH

2. What vehicle did Luke say he'd used to hunt womp rats on Tatooine? ANH

3. What weapons did the Rebels use to penetrate the defenses of the Death Star? ANH

4. What firearm handiwork convinced Obi-Wan that the Empire was behind the death of the Jawas? ANH

5. What was the name of the floating torture device with the hypodermic needle on the Death Star? ANH

6. Why was the escape pod used by C-3PO and R2-D2 not destroyed at the beginning of ANH?

7. Where did Luke keep the rope that he used to swing with Leia across the divide in ANH?

8. What discovery proved to the stormtroopers on Tatooine that "someone was in the pod," and that they were droids? ANH

9. What shape describes the scanner that the Death Star's troops used to check the docked Millennium Falcon for life forms? ANH

The medical droid that attended to Darth Vader at the end of ROS is the same droid that attended to Luke in ESB.

10. What did Luke want to put on Chewbacca before entering the detention area on the Death Star? ANH

11. What did Han tell Chewbacca to do to the deflector shields when they were leaving the Death Star? ANH

12. What color was the other R2 unit seen with R2-D2 on Yavin as the Rebels were discussing the weakness in the Death Star's defenses? ANH

13. As the Death Star was first attacked in ANH, the astro-officer told Darth Vader that the Rebel ships were so small, they were evading which Death Star weapons?

14. How many legs were on the remote probes that landed on Hoth? ESB

15. Why did the Imperial probe droid on Hoth explode? ESB

16. What kind of droid told Luke that evacuating the T-47s would take quite a while? ESB

The stormtroopers' weapons in ANH were slightly modified Sterling 9mm sub-machine guns from the early 1950s. The longer rifles were German MG-34 machine guns.

17. Through what technology did we first see the Imperial walkers? ESB

18. How many blasts did Han fire at Darth Vader when they first met in ESB?

19. What was the name of the band of electromagnetic energy that joined the two small generators on a podracer? TPM

20. What were the Gungans' blue balls of battle energy called? TPM

21. What was the name of the silver protocol droid who greeted the Jedi aboard the Trade Federation battleship? TPM

22. What was the name of the destroyer droids that attacked Qui-Gon and Obi-Wan on the Trade Federation ship near Naboo at the start of TPM?

23. What kind of hyperdrive generator did Watto sell Qui-Gon? TPM

24. What classic cinema spacecraft was seen rusting behind Qui-Gon as he bargains with Watto? TPM

25. What kind of projector did Darth Sidious appear on when he told Nute to "wipe them out?.?.?.?all of them." TPM

26. What were the two colors of the speeder that Anakin used to save Obi-Wan, who was hanging from the flying probe droid? AOC

27. What was used to kill Padmé's unsuccessful assassin, and who used it? AOC

28. How many hover-units were under Yoda's hover chair in the Jedi Temple on Coruscant? AOC

29. What was the name of the droid that was attached to Obi-Wan's personal ships, and what colors did it have? AOC

30. When Anakin headed out to find the Tusken Raiders who abducted his mother, what did the vehicle he used most resemble on Earth? AOC

31. What was Anakin repairing while he asked Padmé why his mother had to die? AOC

32. What was the official name of the little bug-like, cackling droids that landed on Obi-Wan's ship and ripped the top off Arfour? ROS

33. Just before Count Dooku's cruiser began to pitch sideways, what elevator did Anakin (who was carrying an unconscious Obi-Wan) tell R2-D2 to activate? ROS

34. What kind of technological defense did General Grievous use in hallway 328 to thwart the escape of Obi-Wan, Anakin, and Palpatine? ROS

Who Did That?

1. Which of the trained Jedi lost a hand in a Star Wars film?
2. To whom did Anakin/Vader make the offer to rule the Galaxy together?
3. Which characters in which films were seen staring into the twin sunsets of Tatooine?
4. What pilot's call sign was shared by Anakin and Luke?
5. Who attempted to heal or comfort two related characters with a hand on the head in two different films?
6. Which two characters successfully stopped Vader from killing someone with his Force choke?
7. Has there been an amputation in every film?
8. In how many films did characters battle with identical-colored lightsabers?
9. Which characters from ANH made their "debut" in ROS?

George Lucas created one of the most financially successful films ever. Depending on how you calculate earnings, ANH ranks number two to either *Gone with the Wind* (US gross) or *Titanic* (cumulative gross).

In ROS, Obi-Wan picked up Anakin's lightsaber—the same one he later gave to Luke in ANH.

10. Which characters appeared in all six Star Wars films?
11. Which film had the most on-screen lightsaber duels, and who were the losers?
12. Who provided the voice-over for General Grievous's cough?
13. What was the only film in which a leading character using a blue lightsaber was killed by a lightsaber?
14. What was the only film of the six that didn't have a fight between a blue and a red lightsaber?
15. In which film did a Sith lord hold a green lightsaber?
16. Who famously did not earn a medal for heroic actions at the Battle of Yavin?
17. Who nearly caused two Imperial Star Destroyers to collide?
18. Which of the heroes in the original trilogy was the best shot?
19. Who was the only Force ghost to make an appearance in the prequel trilogy?
20. Which characters were seen in the very last frame of ROJ?

Who Said That?

1. Which two characters said, "This is where the fun begins," as they were off on similar missions in their respective film trilogies?
2. In which two films can you hear hairy characters perform the Tarzan yell?
3. Which character had the opening line of ANH and the closing line of ROS?
4. Who had a "bad feeling about this" in ANH, and where?
5. Who had a "bad feeling about this" in ESB, and where?
6. Who had a "bad feeling about this" in ROJ, and where?
7. Who had a "bad feeling about this" in TPM, and where?

ANH has the most swearing, with two *hells* and two *damns*. In the other five films, total, there is just one more of each.

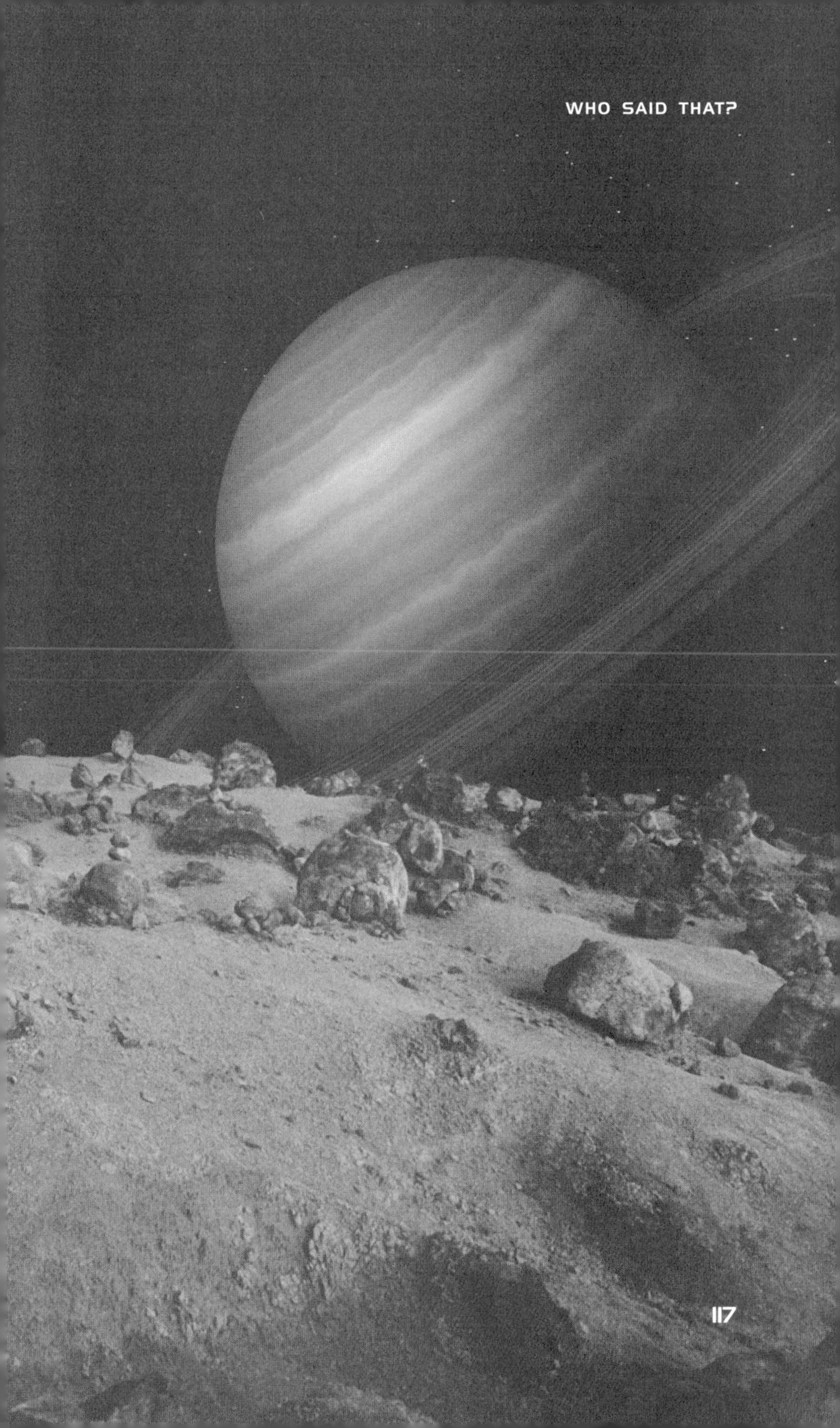

8. Who had a "bad feeling about this" in AOC, and where?
9. Who had a "bad feeling about this" in ROS, and where?
10. Who said, "This deal is getting worse all the time"?
11. Who said, "I'm backwards, you flea-bitten furball!"?
12. Who said, "These Federation types are cowards. The negotiations will be short"?
13. Who said to Luke, "You do not yet realize your importance"?
14. Who said, "I love democracy. I love the Republic"?
15. Who said, "Always a pleasure to meet a Jedi"?
16. Who said, "Why do I get the feeling you're going to be the death of me"?
17. Who said, "The ability to speak does not make you intelligent"?
18. Who said, "No one can kill a Jedi"?
19. Who said, "What a wonderful new smell you've discovered"?
20. Who said the Force was "simple tricks and nonsense"?
21. Who said, "Take care of yourself, Han. I guess that's what you're best at"?

Playwright Tom Stoppard provided uncredited dialog revisions to ROS.

Yoda

1. How did Luke first learn of Yoda?

2. What was Yoda's first comment to Luke? ESB

3. What did Yoda say when Luke said he was looking for a great warrior? ESB

4. Yoda told Luke he needed to do something before he could "meet Yoda." What? ESB

5. What food did Yoda serve Luke in his home? ESB

6. What was Yoda's comment about Luke's eating habits? ESB

7. What was the first reason Yoda gave Obi-Wan that Yoda could not teach Luke? ESB

8. What other reasons did Yoda give for not training Luke? ESB

9. As Yoda was standing on Luke, Luke lost his concentration— what did Yoda scream as he fell? ESB

10. What three things did Yoda say fed the dark side of the Force in ESB?

Yoda's exact species remains a mystery, even to George Lucas.

11. How long had Yoda trained Jedi by the time he met Luke? ESB

12. How did Yoda describe himself to Luke when Luke appeared at his home? ROJ

13. How old did Yoda say he is? ROJ

14. What did Yoda say when Luke said Yoda couldn't die? ROJ

15. What did Yoda say remained before Luke was officially a Jedi? ROJ

16. What would happen, said Yoda, once Luke started down the dark path of anger, fear, and aggression? ROJ

17. What did Yoda feel as he sensed Anakin attacking the Tusken Raiders in AOC?

18. When Yoda told a clone leader to concentrate all fire on the nearest starship, what sector was indicated? AOC

19. How many fingers did Yoda have?

20. What color was the beam on Yoda's lightsaber?

21. In which film was Yoda's first lightsaber battle?

22. What happened when Dooku attacked Yoda with blue force lightning? AOC

23. Whom did Yoda describe as "my old Padawan"? AOC

24. What, said Yoda, is fear of loss? ROS

25. What was Yoda's final advice when Anakin told him about dreams of Padmé's death? ROS

26. While storming the Jedi Temple in ROS, what did Yoda do with his lightsaber that had never been done onscreen before?

27. After the Jedi Temple massacre, what did Yoda counsel Obi-Wan about "the boy you trained"? ROS

28. Finish this sentence from Yoda to Darth Sidious, "Faith in your new apprentice _____." ROS

29. What followed Yoda down, down, down to the bottom of the Senate floor in the end of his fight scene with Darth Sidious? ROS

30. Yoda's appearance was based on two people: Stuart Freeborn, the original makeup artist who designed the character, and which famous wise person?

31. What were Yoda's last words alive?

32. Who spoke first after Yoda died?

During the filming of ESB, puppeteer Frank Oz had to continually remind George Lucas to direct comments to him, and not to the Yoda puppet.

The Answers

Anakin Skywalker

1. He said, in Huttese, "Mel tassa cho-passa." (This translates either to "I was cleaning the fan blades," or "I was cleaning the bin," depending on the source.)
2. "Are you an angel?" In return, she called him a "funny little boy."
3. Qui-Gon, Padmé, Jar Jar, and R2-D2 came to Anakin's home to find shelter from a desert sandstorm.
4. According to his mother, "There was no father. I carried him, I gave birth, I raised him. I can't explain what happened."
5. Shmi Skywalker
6. Obi-Wan found that Anakin's midi-chlorian count was over 20,000-higher even than Master Yoda's.
7. Kitster
8. Qui-Gon gave Anakin this sage advice as Anakin puts on his helmet at the pod race.
9. Sebulba forced Anakin onto the service ramp, which caused Anakin's racer to leap high and over Sebulba's racer.
10. She said, "But you can't stop change any more than you can stop the suns from setting."
11. Aboard Padmé's ship, just as it was leaving Tatooine. TPM
12. In Anakin's first meeting with the Jedi Council, Yoda explained that fear was the path to the dark side ?.?.?.? fear led to anger, anger led to hate, and hate led to suffering. TPM

13. "And you, young Skywalker, we will watch your career with great interest." TPM
14. The beige outfit and brown belt of a Padawan learner
15. He was about to see Padmé, whom he hadn't seen in ten years.
16. He would rival Master Yoda as a swordsman.
17. Attachment and possession were forbidden, but compassion was central to a Jedi's life.
18. On a garden terrace at Padmé's Naboo lake retreat. AOC
19. Negotiations with a lightsaber
20. He saw his mother suffering and in pain, which led to Anakin and Padmé leaving for Tatooine.
21. A cutting machine on the giant battle droid assembly line sliced off an important part.
22. His right arm was cut off in the lightsaber duel with Count Dooku. AOC
23. A shiny gold arm
24. R2-D2 and C-3PO
25. He expected that Anakin would be older. Anakin replied that he thought General Grievous would be taller.
26. "Open all hatches, and extend all flaps and drag fins."
27. On Padmé's ship, just as Anakin was leaving Tatooine for the first time in TPM.
28. On the condition that Anakin would not be promoted to Master.
29. It was against the Jedi code, the Republic, a mentor, and a friend (Palpatine). ROS
30. Yes. When Vader killed Obi-Wan in ANH, there was balance in the Force-the Jedi and the Sith each had one remaining Master and apprentice. (Emperor/Vader and Yoda/Luke). After Vader

killed the Emperor and died in ROJ, there were no more Sith in the film universe, bringing another kind of balance to the Force.

31. "I pledge myself to your teachings." ROS

32. He said, "What have I done?" before falling back and dropping his lightsaber.

33. He strangled his wife.

34. He lost a left arm and both legs by Obi-Wan's lightsaber, then he caught fire as he slid into the magma. He also lost his family. It was a bad day all around.

35. So Anakin could look on Luke with his own eyes.

36. "You were right about me. Tell your sister you were right."

The Bad Guys

1. Imperial stormtroopers searching for C-3PO and R2-D2

2. Governor Tarkin and Grand Moff Tarkin

3. Four

4. The Imperial Senate

5. Viceroy Nute Gunray (with the three-pointed crown), Captain Daultay Dofine (with the long straight hat) and the Viceroy's adviser, Rune Haako (with the more round hat). They were from the planet Neimoidia.

6. "Stunted slime."

7. Camp Four

8. He appeared behind Darth Sidious in a transmission to Nute and Rune.

9. Red, of course

10. Three

11. Only once, and only because Obi-Wan had just struck a fatal blow to his midsection.

12. Shooting at Anakin's pod racer mid-race, and then celebrating a direct hit.

13. Always two: a master and an apprentice. TPM

14. Her name was Zam. Zam Wessell, a shapeshifting Clawdite bounty hunter from the planet Zolan.

15. Count Dooku and Viceroy Nute Gunray

16. Boba Fett, the bounty hunter and son of Jango Fett, the clone host, died on Tatooine when the Sarlacc in the Pit of Carkoon began digesting him for a thousand years. But in nonfilm Star Wars stories, he survived this.

17. Tyranus did, on one of the moons of Bogden

18. Seismic charges

19. Nute Gunray

20. The Techno Council, the Banking Clan, and the Trade Federation

21. "We must persuade the Commerce Guild and the Corporate Alliance to sign the treaty." AOC

22. Dooku was a Jedi knight.

23. Jango Fett

24. He was beheaded by Mace Windu's lightsaber in the Geonosis arena. AOC

25. He knelt to pick up his father's helmet in the arena.

26. The designs for the ultimate weapon—the unbuilt Death Star—seen as a red hologram.

27. General Grievous

28. There are heroes on both sides. Evil is everywhere.

29. Vulture droids

30. Eight, but not for long. ROS

31. "Fire the emergency booster engines!"
32. It was elevator 31174, and its roof got cut open by Anakin's lightsaber.
33. Palpatine saying, "Do it." ROS
34. General Grievous. ROS
35. To Mustafar
36. In the outer rim
37. He could create life with midi-chlorians, and save people from death. ROS
38. His apprentice killed him in his sleep. ROS
39. An organic brain and nervous system, and organic yellow eyes. Grievous had once been a Kaleesh warlord, and became a cyborg when a bomb destroyed a ship he was on. EU
40. On Utapau, Obi-Wan shot him in his organic guts. The blasts caused Grievous to short circuit and catch fire.
41. The clones
42. Captain Kargi

Behind the Scenes

1. George Lucas took the name "Anakin" from his friend and fellow film director, Ken Annakin.
2. NOMINATED (10) Best picture, Supporting Actor (Alec Guinness), Direction, Original Screenplay, Costume Design, WON (5) Art Direction, Sound, Film Editing, Visual Effects, Original Score. Ben Burtt also got a Special Achievement Award for sound effects creation.
3. NOMINATED (3) Art Direction, Original Score. WON (1) Sound, Dennis Muren, Brian Johnson, Richard Ed Lund, and Bruce

Nicholson also got a Special Achievement Award for visual effects.

4. 15

5. Darth Vader was ranked number 3, behind Dr. Hannibal Lecter and Norman Bates.

6. "May the Force be with you" was ranked number 8.

7. Han Solo was ranked number 14, and Obi-Wan Kenobi was ranked number 37.

8. Ewan McGregor said it in *Entertainment Weekly*.

9. Mark Hamill had been in a serious car accident and suffered facial damage at the end of the filming of *A New Hope*. Incorporating Hamill's new face into the storyline addressed any possible questions.

10. R2-D2 and other radio-controlled robots were badly damaged in a pile up when they picked up Tunisian Air Force Transmission.

11. The director, Richard Marquand and the producer, Howard Kazanjian were at the helm.

12. He said he repeated common phonetic sounds until he discovered one he liked.

13. It was the first *Star Wars* film that was not the top grossing film internationally the year it was released. (*Spider-Man*, *Harry Potter 2* and *Lord of the Rings: The Two Towers* all had higher international gross receipts.)

14. Christian Hayden wore the suit. It was fitted with lifts so he could reach the appropriate height.

15. It was called *Revenge of the Jedi* until a few weeks before release.

16. Five. ANH, ESB, and ROJ each won. TPM and AOC were nominated. ROS was passed by.

17. It was in 1980, just prior to the release of *The Empire Strikes Back*, which was always billed as Episode V.

18. He wasn't. Whether he was being noble or hedging his bets against a possible flop, Jones's name didn't appear until the film was re-released in 1997.

19. Brian DePalma

20. 1978, 1979, 1981, 1982, and 1997.

21. The design for the Millennium Falcon.

22. Lucas had said that he only wanted unknowns in the three lead roles.

23. ESB

24. 40. According to a few sources, it broke attendance records in 39 of those 40 theaters.

25. Denis Lawson, who played Wedge in the original trilogy, is the uncle of Ewan McGregor.

26. All the Imperial military characters were wearing uniforms which had the insignia of an Imperial Navy commander.

27. The story didn't have a beginning or an end; it depended on ANH for its beginning, and ROJ for its end.

28. David Lynch and David Cronenberg

29. His friend Steven Spielberg, who was a member of the Director's Guild, and so could not work on a non-union film.

30. Blue Harvest was the fake name used by the crew of ROJ (with T-shirts and everything) in order to keep the shooting location a secret and to keep location prices from rising.

31. That Darth Vader would be unmasked, and another actor would be inside.

32. To give Frank Oz and the three other puppeteers enough space to bring the Yoda puppet to life.

33. It was ranked number one—it was supposedly the greatest film score of all time.
34. It was Tunisia's first major rainstorm, which wrecked the set of Luke's home.
35. ROJ. The Yuma Desert in Arizona stood in for Tatooine, and Endor scenes were shot in the forests near Crescent City, California.
36. In the lobby of their Norwegian hotel, filming Hamill who was outside the window

C-3PO

1. "Oh, oh. Where is everybody?"
2. R2-D2 told C-3PO that he was naked and his parts were showing. TPM
3. R2-D2 called C-3PO a mindless philosopher.
4. "The damage doesn't look as bad from out here."
5. A nearby explosion
6. His joints were almost frozen.
7. If the Jawas would melt the droids down
8. Over six million forms of communication
9. Programming binary load lifters
10. The maker
11. "Shut down all garbage mashers on the detention level!"
12. To maintenance
13. Any of C-3PO's circuits or gears
14. The deck officer
15. "Stupid little short circuit."
16. A human being

17. That the hyperdrive motivator was damaged, and going to light speed would be impossible

18. 3,720 to 1

19. We'll never know. Leia told him to shut up before we heard the answer.

20. Short circuit

21. He knocks.

22. "Toota odd mishka Jabba du Hutt."

23. To His Excellency's (Jabba's) main audience chamber

24. Jabba licking his lips and pulling Leia closer

25. C-3PO's "divine influence."

26. "I have decided that we shall stay here."

27. Seeing "machines creating machines."

28. A battle droid

29. "I'm programmed for etiquette, not destruction!" AOC

30. To have C-3PO's mind wiped

31. Mel Blanc, whom you may remember as just about every Looney Tunes character.

Chewbacca

1. Bears, dogs, lions, tigers, and walruses

2. Peter Mayhew got his break in acting after having been featured in a newspaper article about the men with the biggest feet in England.

3. Chewbacca was a Wookiee.

4. He was the co-pilot and the chief mechanic.

5. Slightly over seven feet, two inches tall, since that's how tall Peter Mayhew was.

6. Human, with long sideburns. Some will argue that Obi-Wan had met Chewbacca before. And some will not.

7. His left shoulder

8. He clonked his head on a pair of hanging dice. This was the only scene in any of the films where the dice were seen.

9. Eight

10. They pulled people's arms out of their sockets.

11. He locked in the auxiliary power.

12. Jam its transmissions

13. Welding glasses, in addition to his usual ammunition belt

14. The hydrospanner

15. Fuzzball

16. The transfer circuits

17. He put the droid's head on backwards.

18. They played "keep away" with C-3PO's head.

19. One of them dropped it while they were tossing it to each other.

20. 25,000

21. Because he didn't fit well. Han explained that the Empire didn't design it with Wookiees in mind.

22. "Fly casual."

23. Chewbacca blasted him off his speeder with his crossbow laser weapon.

24. One soldier was pulled out by Chewbacca and thrown to the ground; the other was knocked unconscious by the Ewoks.

25. ROS

26. George Lucas's dog, Indiana, who was also the namesake of Indiana Jones, the Steven Spielberg film series in which George Lucas was a producer.

27. Chewbacca had been sold into slavery, and Solo was an

Imperial lieutenant who wouldn't carry out a death order on Chewbacca. As the two escaped, they both got a bounty on their heads, and became smugglers.

Darth Vader

1. "Thank you, my master." ROS
2. Captain Antilles and Admiral Motti
3. That the crew of the Millennium Falcon was returning the stolen plans to Leia.
4. He didn't say. After saying he had not felt it since?.?.?.? he turned and walked away. But we all know he meant Obi-Wan.
5. Escape. Vader meant that it was Obi-Wan's intention to face his old student.
6. "I've been waiting for you, Obi-Wan. We meet at last."
7. Weak
8. It was the day Obi-Wan Kenobi died, he thought it would be the day Rebellion ended.
9. It was the day the Death Star was destroyed.
10. It was on backwards.
11. He kicked Obi-Wan's cloak with his foot, seemingly confused.
12. Because cheating death was a knowledge either unknown or forgotten by the Sith.
13. They were fighters who had broken off from the main group.
14. Finding Luke Skywalker
15. He dispatched thousands of remote probes throughout the Galaxy.
16. Black on the outside, off-white on the inside, as seen on Life Supports of the Rich and Famous. And ESB.

17. Vader's skin—the back of his head, to be precise.

18. Monitors and controls

19. Coming out of lightspeed too close to the Hoth system where the Rebels were.

20. "What is thy bidding, my master?"

21. Vader put up his hand and absorbed the blasts easily. Then Vader drew the blaster to him using the Force.

22. "We would be honored if you would join us."

23. Vader wanted to test the freezing process so he could deliver Luke Skywalker the same way.

24. "The Force is with you, young Skywalker. But you are not a Jedi yet." ESB

25. That Luke would destroy the Emperor.

26. Luke

27. Luke rolled down the stairs. Vader jumped.

28. ROS

29. Yes, in ESB, in the carbon freezing scene, C-3PO and Darth Vader were together again for the last time.

30. The stand-in line was "You don't know the truth. Obi-Wan killed your father." James Earl Jones replaced it with the actual line in post-production.

31. To put the construction of the Death Star back on schedule.

32. "Perhaps I can find new ways to motivate them."

33. "The Death Star will be completed on time."

34. To protect them from the Emperor. ESB

35. His compassion for his father.

36. When Boba Fett aimed his rifle at Chewbacca in the carbon freezing chamber in ESB, Vader pushed the rifle away.

37. "The Emperor has been expecting you."

38. He said Luke's skills were complete, and that Luke was indeed powerful.

39. Vader said he would kill Luke if that were Luke's destiny.

40. He threw his lightsaber toward Luke, striking a support that caused the bridge Luke was standing on to crash down.

41. He shrugged. And then he started setting detonators.

42. He read Luke's mind.

43. Vader groaned. Wouldn't you?

44. He found out during the screening at an early screening of ANH.

45. James Earl Jones

46. James Earl Jones reprised his role as Vader's voice.

47. "Where is Padmé?"

48. "No!"

The Death Star

1. A battle station and an exceptionally powerful weapon

2. The tractor beam

3. The circular disk that held the Death Star's awesome laser.

4. Four

5. Grand Moff Tarkin (Moff is short for Military Officer.)

6. They opened the magnetic field.

7. They wore stormtrooper uniforms.

8. 2

9. TK-421

10. 1138

11. Cameras and laser gate controls

12. 2187—a number that was also the name of a short film from Canada that was important to Lucas.

13. 5

14. Hexagonal

15. 3263827

16. R2-D2 found it by plugging into the Death Star's computer.

17. On earlier versions of ANH, it said, "Power," and "Tractor Beam" in English, a language that was not read or written a long time ago in a galaxy far, far away. There, they wrote in Basic. The words were later changed digitally.

18. A power loss at any one of the terminals would let the ship leave.

19. At maximum velocity

20. Red Leader (known in the novel as Garven Dreis)

21. "Stand by."

22. Certain death

23. It was protected by an energy shield on the Endor surface.

24. Three

25. Seven

26. The one on the north tower

27. Green

28. Fully armed and functional

29. The red hologram of its basic design was seen on Geonosis in AOC, as introduced by Poggle the Lesser.

Emperor Palpatine

1. Darth Vader

2. On Naboo, after the battle of Naboo. TPM

3. Anakin would become invincible.
4. Obi-Wan, Anakin, and Palpatine were all killed on a Death Star.
5. When Obi-Wan was trapped and suspended in a blue force field, Count Dooku explained that the Republic was in the hands of a Sith Lord named Darth Sidious. AOC
6. In ROJ, Palpatine urged Luke to kill a defeated Darth Vader, but was denied. In ROS, Palpatine convinced Anakin to kill Dooku. See what happens when you listen to Palpatine?
7. The wish to continue the search for Luke.
8. Darth Vader was to bring Luke to the Emperor because Luke had grown too strong, and it would take both Sith Lords to turn Luke to the dark side.
9. That they could be a threat to the Emperor.
10. The Emperor said he had not felt Luke's presence, and wondered if Vader's feelings were clear on the matter.
11. "Welcome, young Skywalker, I have been expecting you."
12. "According to my design."
13. Luke's friends on the Sanctuary Moon, as well as the Rebel fleet.
14. Luke's "pitiful little band."
15. His lack of vision.
16. To two: First to Anakin in ROS, and then to Luke in ROJ.
17. None of them. He's seen in all but ANH, in which "the Emperor" was mentioned.
18. To be a Jedi Master, as Palpatine's personal representative on the Jedi Council.
19. To be the eyes, ears, and voice of the Republic.
20. That the Jedi Council wanted to betray Palpatine, overthrow the government, and control the Republic.
21. Embrace a larger view of the Force.

22. Treason
23. Mace Windu. (Perhaps that's how he got his name?)
24. Mace Windu's lightsaber redirected Palpatine's Force lightning back to Palpatine, creating a powerful "superconducting loop" that terribly disfigured Palpatine's face. ROS
25. Order 66
26. "Now, young Skywalker, you will die!" Then the Emperor died instead. ROJ

The Galactic Republic

1. With thunderous applause.
2. The Galactic Republic and, after its death, it became known as the Old Republic.
3. Coruscant
4. The Supreme Chancellor
5. Because of the taxation of trade routes to outlying star systems.
6. The Supreme Chancellor
7. Endlessly debating the alarming chain of events
8. The planet was Naboo, and the ruler was Queen Amidala.
9. Lord Darth Sidious and Senator Palpatine, who were actually one and the same.
10. "The Chair recognizes the Senator from the sovereign system of Naboo."
11. Supreme Chancellor Valorum was actually the ranking individual in the entire Galaxy until somebody took his job.
12. Palpatine
13. Several thousand solar systems had declared their intentions to leave the Republic.

14. The mysterious Count Dooku

15. The creation of an Army of the Republic.

16. The Military Creation Act

17. The Trade Federations or the Commerce Guilds

18. Nute Gunray remained viceroy of the Trade Federation, signaling that the Senate was powerless.

19. Senator Jar Jar Binks of Naboo

20. To authorize an army of clone warriors to create the Republic's first standing army.

21. "That's the day we lose democracy."

22. That the Republic would be reorganized into the first Galactic Empire?.?.?.? for a safe and secure society.

23. The smaller, Emperor-dominated Imperial Senate.

24. Princess Leia, a member of the Imperial Senate from Alderaan, appears in the opening scene of ANH.

Han Solo

1. "Wonderful girl. Either I'm going to kill her, or I'm beginning to like her."

2. At the cantina in Mos Eisley on Tatooine. ANH

3. Ten thousand up front

4. Seventeen thousand. Two thousand up front, and fifteen thousand at Alderaan.

5. The fans objected, that's what happened. In the 1977 release, Han shot first. But George Lucas later changed the scene to make Han appear less cold-blooded, and raised an uproar. The 2004 DVD now shows Han shooting just barely before Greedo.

6. A meteor shower; an asteroid collision

7. "Hokey religions and ancient weapons."
8. "More wealth than you can imagine."
9. A lot
10. More like suicide
11. "Boring conversation anyway."
12. The compactor room was magnetically sealed.
13. The bounty hunter he ran into on Ord Mantell.
14. Your Highnessness
15. Han's tauntaun dropped dead.
16. After cutting one open, he said, "And I thought they smelled bad on the outside."
17. He put Luke's body inside the dead tauntaun. ESB
18. To pull the ears off a gundark.
19. Striking Vader's ship just before Vader could fire on Luke at the Death Star in ANH.
20. "Take care of yourself." Luke replied with, "You too."
21. "Set 2-7-1."
22. "I'm a nice man."
23. "I feel terrible."
24. His hands were tied going in, but freed and grasping outward in the frozen state.
25. One year
26. Carbonite
27. "Someone who loves you."
28. He got "sidetracked."
29. Temporary blindness. ROJ
30. "I'm out of it for a little while and everybody gets delusions of grandeur."
31. Han called Jabba a "slimy piece of worm-ridden filth."
32. General

33. He made a noise stepping on a stick.
34. Cuddle Han and purr
35. Rebel scum.
36. He "hot-wires the thing."
37. They marry and have three children: twins Jacen and Jaina, and then Anakin, named for his grandfather.

Jabba the Hutt

1. Greedo
2. Lucas was unsatisfied with the special effects capabilities in 1977, but happy with computer graphics capabilities in 1997.
3. To Boba Fett in ESB
4. After Darth Vader had captured Luke Skywalker. ESB
5. Yellow-Red
6. First Han (who started the whole rescue mission), then Lando, then the droids, then Chewbacca with Leia, and finally Luke.
7. A talking mechanical arm with an electronic eye.
8. "Exalted One."
9. Jabba got angry with it and disintegrated it.
10. Oola
11. He reached into a bowl of water and took out a small, live, screaming animal to eat.
12. He swatted C-3PO and sent him hurtling backward.
13. Bib Fortuna
14. The Rancor
15. He was swallowed by the Rancor.
16. Jabba's platform rolled back to reveal a caged hole in the floor for spectators.

17. Bantha fodder
18. Leia strangled him with the chain Jabba attached between them.
19. Jabba's luxury sail barge was called the Khetanna, and it was made by Ubrikkian Industries and no, it's not mentioned in any films.
20. Salacious Crumb
21. The all-powerful Sarlacc
22. Himself

Jar Jar Binks

1. Gungan
2. "It's demanded by the Gods," said Jar Jar, and later it was described by Qui-Gon as a "life-debt."
3. Jar Jar referred to it as Gunga City, but officially the city was called Otoh Gunga.
4. Captain Tarpals
5. Through the planet core.
6. It was the manta-like Gungan transport that brought Qui-Gon, Obi-Wan, and Jar Jar to the Naboo capital.
7. "Maxi-big, da Force."
8. Hit the nose.
9. They went to the sacred place—the ruins of the Gungan Sacred Temple. TPM
10. "Ouch time."
11. He had snared a piece of fruit from a fruit bowl with his tongue.
12. It got zapped by the energy binders in Anakin's podracer.
13. "My tongue is fat!"

14. He called it a grand army, and he thought that the Gungan army was why the Naboo people didn't like the Gungans.
15. Bombad General
16. He faints.
17. Boss Nass
18. For bringing the Gungans and the Naboo together.
19. "Steady. Steady."
20. It was a kaadu.
21. The droid's blaster fired randomly, and several other battle droids got blasted by mistake.

The Jedi Order

1. Han used Luke's lightsaber when he cut open the tauntaun to keep Luke warm inside.
2. The Jedi Council
3. A blast shield
4. In Obi-Wan's home. Obi-Wan gave it to him.
5. Han in pain in the Cloud City, in ESB.
6. His "first steps into a larger world"
7. He felt "a tremor in the force."
8. On a few laser blasts fired by an Imperial stormtrooper on a speeder bike, and then on the front of the speeder bike itself.
9. Jinn
10. Qui-Gon Jinn and Obi-Wan Kenobi
11. Obi-Wan Kenobi was a Padawan, or student.
12. The destroyer droids rolled down a hallway before opening into battle position. They used shield generators, a type of force field, to defend themselves.

13. They exited via the ventilation shaft.
14. It was Qui-Gon's dying wish that Obi-Wan train Anakin. TPM
15. Coruscant
16. "We're keepers of the peace, not soldiers."
17. "Go back to your drinks."
18. They were younglings, and the ones on-screen were about four years old.
19. Sifo-Dyas
20. Oddball
21. To Boz Pity
22. Because they needed Anakin more than Anakin knew, which was an allusion to the Prophecy.
23. The Wookiees'
24. The Senate, and not to its leader (who had managed to stay in office long after his term had expired).
25. Anakin said the Sith thought inwards, only about themselves, but the Jedi were selfless, only caring about others.
26. Yoda said it to Mace Windu and Obi-Wan on the transport. (Before that, Mace did say, "May the Force be with us all.")
27. He felt that Palpatine had become too powerful.
28. Yoda had sensed the killings elsewhere, so he was ready for his attackers and got them first. On Utapau, Obi-Wan was the first Jedi to be fired upon. The blast missed, causing him to drop off a cliff into water, but he survived.
29. To dismantle the coded signal which told the Jedi to return to the Jedi Temple.
30. It was an ancient legend, believed by the Jedi, which predicted one person would restore balance to the Force, most likely by destroying the Sith.
31. ROJ

32. No, Yoda said it was a prophecy that misread could have been.
ROS

33. Bogan

34. The light side

Lando Calrissian

1. She thought Han was talking about a star system called Lando.

2. Cardplayer, gambler, scoundrel. ESB

3. Bespin. ESB

4. A tibanna gas mine. ESB

5. Han said Lando conned somebody out of it.

6. There were two, and they were reddish in color.

7. A slimy, double-crossing, no-good swindler.

8. He's "the administrator of this facility." ESB

9. He kissed her hand.

10. The mine was small, not self-sufficient, and there were supply and labor problems.

11. They were not part of the mining guild or under the Empire's jurisdiction. Therefore, it was an illegal operation.

12. The Empire had threatened to close down Lando's mining business.

13. Leave a garrison of soldiers on the Cloud City.

14. He put on his cape and he left.

15. He contacted Lobot, his assistant, via a wrist communicator.

16. A rifle with a very large bayonet.

17. The Sarlacc

18. "No, wait, I thought you were blind!"

19. General

20. The Battle of Taanab
21. Perhaps he was asked, said Han, but he "ain't crazy" and besides, Lando was the "respectable" one.
22. Get a scratch.
23. Or this would be the shortest offensive of all time.
24. Lando realized that if he couldn't read the shield's status, the Empire must have been jamming them, which meant the Empire was expecting the attack.
25. To move closer to the Imperial Star Destroyers and engage them at point-blank range.
26. Red Group and Gold Group
27. Gold
28. The Millennium Falcon scraping against the side of the Death Star and losing some equipment.

Luke Skywalker

1. Kill Obi-Wan. ANH
2. Scream "NO!" at Obi-Wan's death, and run into the Millennium Falcon. ANH
3. As Luke was about to take off to destroy the Death Star, Obi-Wan said, "Run, Luke, run!"
4. He was a moisture farmer.
5. Because Owen needed Luke to stay on the farm for one more season.
6. Uncle Owen had said that Anakin had been a navigator on a spice freighter.
7. To Tosche Station
8. Power converters

9. Three or four seasons

10. A garbage masher

11. Their skeletons, and their home on fire.

12. As easy as bulls-eyeing womp rats.

13. Beggar's Canyon

14. It was a carnivorous, abominable snowman-type of creature, called a Wampa.

15. Echo Three

16. "You smell something?"

17. Luke was dragged by his left leg into the Wampa's cave.

18. Commander

19. A meteorite

20. Rogue Leader

21. Dack

22. Dack had no approach pattern.

23. The detonator he used to destroy a walker soon after.

24. Luke summoned his lightsaber to fly out of a snow bank and into his hand.

25. He saw Boba Fett leading the procession with Han's frozen body.

26. His son was born.

27. That Luke had returned to Tatooine to save Han from Jabba the Hutt.

28. That the Galactic Empire had begun to build an even more powerful Death Star.

29. As a Jedi knight and friend to Captain Solo.

30. To bargain for Solo's life.

31. Daytime

32. In ROJ, as Luke entered Jabba's palace, the first guards he encountered stepped back against the wall, clutching their throats.

33. That Jabba could either profit by Luke's offer, or be destroyed.
34. A bone, to prop its mouth open, and then the dungeon door, which dropped and killed it.
35. From Jabba's sail barge. R2-D2 launched it from an opening in his head.
36. "Let's go, and don't forget the droids." ROJ
37. In a conversation with the Force ghost of Obi-Wan on Dagobah, soon after Yoda died.
38. Because though the feelings do Luke credit, they could be used to serve the Emperor.
39. He sensed Vader was on the nearby Star Destroyer, and realized he was endangering the mission.
40. "I'm endangering the mission."
41. "Father."
42. His overconfidence
43. Luke's faith in his friends
44. Two stormtroopers got on with Luke, and Darth Vader alone got off with him.
45. "The final destruction of the Rebel Alliance, and the end of your insignificant Rebellion."
46. Two. Mark Hamill and the baby Aiden Barton in ROS.

The Millennium Falcon

1. Point five past light speed
2. The Kessel Run
3. Docking Bay 94
4. Two
5. The navi-computer

6. The Falcon came out of hyperspace.
7. In the area where Alderaan used to be
8. The Death Star
9. Because the Death Star was pulling it in with a tractor beam.
10. Docking bay "twenty-three-seven" (2037)
11. Several escape pods
12. In the hidden cargo holds used for smuggling.
13. TK-421. In the novel, he was THX-1138.
14. The B-29 Superfortress bomber
15. It was a YT-1300 Corellian freighter/transport, though its two most recent owners had upgraded it significantly.
16. The power coupling on the negative axis had been polarized.
17. Mynocks
18. Eat the power cables.
19. Platform 3-2-7
20. It became Princess Leia's ship.
21. Lando told co-pilot Nien to lock onto the strongest power source.
22. He said he had a funny feeling, like he was not going to see his ship again.
23. Yes. It survived the attack on the Death Star, but just barely.
24. In Blade Runner, as the Hero Spinner aircraft was about to land, a Pan Am sign blinks in the upper left corner. The camera pans directly over a model of the Falcon serving as the dark, pointed top of a skyscraper.

Obi-Wan Kenobi

1. Obi-Wan said, "I have a bad feeling about this" in TPM.
2. Beyond the Dune Sea

3. A wizard and a crazy old man

4. He made a monster sound (technically, he was impersonating a Krayt dragon).

5. She called Obi-Wan "General Kenobi."

6. "There are alternatives to fighting."

7. "The fool, or the fool who follows him?" asked Obi-Wan of Han inside the Death Star.

8. "Your destiny lies along a different path than mine. The Force will be with you always."

9. He disabled the tractor beam so the Millennium Falcon could escape.

10. Obi-Wan would become more powerful than Vader could possibly imagine.

11. He raised his lightsaber toward the sky, allowing Darth Vader to strike him down with a lightsaber.

12. To allow the escape of the Millennium Falcon from the Death Star.

13. Obi-Wan explained that the seduction of the dark side destroyed the good man that was Luke's father.

14. Our own point of view.

15. "I was wrong."

16. More machine than man?.?.?.? twisted and evil

17. When Luke told Obi-Wan he couldn't kill his own father. ROJ

18. Obi-Wan was born in 57 BBY (Before the Battle of Yavin, the Star Wars year when the Death Star was destroyed), and so he was 57 in ANH. Sir Alec Guinness was 62.

19. "Hello, there."

20. "Another pathetic life form." TPM

21. Nothing. Obi-Wan simply smiled and shook hands, although R2-D2 beeped a lot. TPM

22. Obi-Wan sliced Darth Maul in half with Qui-Gon's lightsaber.
23. "Confer on you the level of Jedi Knight, the council does." TPM
24. He had returned from a border dispute on Ansion. AOC
25. A nest of gundarks
26. According to Anakin, Obi-Wan fell in and Anakin rescued him.
27. They were politicians, who were not to be trusted, and that they focus only on pleasing those who fund their campaigns.
28. Death sticks
29. Go home and rethink your life.
30. Obi-Wan had Arfour jettison his ship's spare parts canisters, and the guided missile impacted with them.
31. An unusual concentration of Federation ships
32. Flying
33. Obi-Wan ejected out of his ship, did a backflip, and cut down four battle droids with his lightsaber.
34. "Not to worry. We are still flying half a ship."
35. Obi-Wan said it was the ninth time, and that the business on Cato Neimoidia didn't count.
36. To spy on Palpatine and report on his dealings.
37. The Younglings. ROS
38. He had stowed away on Padmé's ship when she flew to find him.
39. Obi-Wan said, "You were my brother. I loved you."
40. R2-D2, C-3PO, and Padmé
41. Yoda told Obi-Wan to learn to commune with Qui-Gon, who had returned from the netherworld of the Force and had learned how to become a Force ghost.

Original Trilogy Characters

1. C-3PO said, "Did you hear that?"
2. Chewbacca growled at the end of the award ceremony, possibly about not getting a medal.
3. Biggs Darklighter
4. They were killed by Imperial stormtroopers.
5. General Jan Dodonna
6. A Jawa who seemed to like touching it.
7. The bartender
8. They burned the bodies.
9. Three
10. The best bush pilot in the outer rim territories
11. "Cut the chatter, Red Two."
12. Luke Skywalker
13. A tauntaun
14. Until the energy shields were activated.
15. In ROJ, in Jabba's palace, on Tatooine
16. Five
17. Lobot
18. Ugnaughts
19. Wedge Antilles
20. Ubese
21. Boushh
22. A thermal detonator
23. It thwaps an insect with its very long tongue, and then burps.
24. Metal spikes
25. Leia
26. The Rancor had four claws on each hand.

27. They would be slowly digested over a thousand years, and thus learn a new definition of pain.

28. In ROJ, Han accidentally ignited Boba Fett's jetpack with a spear. The bounty hunter then flew and crashed into Jabba's sail barge before rolling into the deadly Pit of Carkoon.

29. Mon Mothma

30. Admiral Ackbar, of the species Mon Calamari

31. General Lando Calrissian

32. General Madine explained that they'd stolen a small Imperial shuttle.

33. General Han Solo

34. Never

35. In the credits of ROJ

36. It sat down beside her for a moment on a fallen tree, until she removed her helmet.

37. R2-D2 produced a circular saw and the group dropped hard onto the ground.

38. When they saw C-3PO for the first time, he was mistaken for a god.

39. He's going to be the main course at a dinner in C-3PO's honor.

40. Nien Nunb was a puppet performed by Mike Quinn and Richard Bonehill. Kipsang Rotich from Kenya spoke for Nien in his native language, Haya.

41. Home One

42. They were both played by Kenny Baker.

43. Wedge Antilles, who had flown on every mission in ANH, ESB, and ROJ.

44. Stormtrooper helmets

45. Luke got shot in his mechanical hand, then Leia got hit in the shoulder, and finally Darth Vader lost his own mechanical hand to Luke.

Padmé Amidala

1. Star Trek
2. Queen Amidala
3. 14
4. A red Scar of Remembrance divided her lower lip, and red beauty marks were placed on each cheek.
5. White. Evidently, white polish on thumbnails is a tradition in Padmé's corner of Naboo.
6. Captain Panaka
7. On the outskirts
8. Because it was a trick that would help the Trade Federation to find her.
9. Their overthrow of her planet wouldn't be considered legal until they had her signature.
10. Queen Jamillia. AOC
11. Sio Bibble
12. To unite with the undersea Gungans and put aside years of animosity.
13. Theed
14. They stepped onto a lower window ledge and fired cables at the upper ledge. Once secure, the cables pulled their passengers upward to the higher window ledge, and they climbed in and ultimately defeated the Neimodians.
15. She became a popular and outspoken member of the Galactic Senate.
16. Cordé
17. Captain Gregar Typho, the nephew of Captain Panaka, wore a simple eyepatch because he lost an eye in the Battle of Naboo.

18. Kouhuns

19. The Separatists would bring violence in return.

20. Dormé

21. "No. I shouldn't have done that." AOC

22. His name was Palo, he had dark curly hair and dreamy eyes, and he became an artist. AOC

23. Another massive animal, much like a pterodactyl, emerged from the sea near Kamino's floating Tipoca City, bringing a rider toward the buildings in the rain.

24. She knelt beside him lovingly, she rocked him, and she stroked his hair.

25. She was scratched on the back by the cat-like Nexu.

26. It was identical to the hair of her daughter, Princess Leia, in the first scene (and the rest of) ANH.

27. She doubted the current queen would allow her to continue in the Senate, and she said the council would expel Anakin.

28. To ask Palpatine to stop the fighting and let diplomacy resume.

29. Obi-Wan, in Anakin's dreams of Padmé's death.

30. Her will to live. ROS

31. Luke

32. Padmé was holding the wooden pendant Anakin gave her in her funeral procession.

33. He told Darth Vader that Vader killed her.

34. Yes. In AOC she met Beru and Owen Lars on Tatooine, and in ROS she sat with Bail Organa in the Senate as the Republic became an Empire, though she never met Bail's wife Breha.

35. Yes, because it was Padmé whose vote of no confidence (in AOC) caused Palpatine to rise to become Chancellor, and it was Padmé's impending death that inspired Anakin to join the dark side (and Darth Sidious) to protect her.

The Planets

1. A long time ago in a galaxy far, far away
2. Tatooine
3. Alderaan
4. On Yavin's fourth moon
5. Dantooine
6. Hoth
7. To fill a space cruiser
8. Massive life-form readings. ESB
9. Luke called Yoda's home a slimy mudhole.
10. Anoat
11. The Dagobah System, to see Yoda
12. The forest moon of Endor
13. Sullust
14. On the Sanctuary Moon
15. On Endor: First with Ewok cheers, and later with fireworks.
16. Coruscant
17. The entire planet was one big city.
18. Palpatine was originally from Naboo. TPM
19. The Rishi Maze
20. Battle droids
21. The Wookiees lived on Kashyyyk, and Yoda went because "good relations with the Wookiees I have."
22. In the Utapau system
23. The Mustafar system
24. It was a lava mining facility and smelting operation
25. Besbin (Lando's Cloud City), Tatooine, Naboo (where a Gungan (possibly Jar Jar) was yelling "We'sa Free"), and Coruscant

Prequel Trilogy Characters

1. Watto

2. Watto's lower left tooth is broken.

3. Red and blue

4. His name was Sebulba, and he was a Dug.

5. The right head (which is on the viewer's left)

6. Boles Roor

7. Ody Mandrell, with his record-setting pit droid team

8. Sebulba called Anakin "bantha fodder" (translated from Huttese) just before the pod race in TPM, which was what Jabba said Luke would also become in ROJ.

9. Quadrinero's

10. Poo-doo!

11. Bail Antilles of Alderaan and Ainlee Teem of Malastare

12. Depending on your meaning of the word "word," Boss Nass said "peace," then Jar Jar said "Yahoo," and finally R2-D2 beeped happily.

13. 10 years. TPM took place in the Star Wars year 32 BBY, and AOC took place in 22 BBY. (That's Before the Battle of Yalta, during which took place the events in ANH.)

14. Dex, also known as Dexter Jettster of Dex's Diner

15. He had seen darts like that on Subterrel, beyond the Outer Rim, where he had been prospecting long ago. He said the darts belonged to "them cloners."

16. How good your manners are, and how big your pocketbook is.

17. Lama Su

18. Clones can think creatively.

19. Jango Fett, the bounty hunter, and the "father" of the unaltered clone, Boba Fett.

20. Picking the mushrooms that grow on the vaporators.
21. Cliegg Lars, father of Owen Lars, who raised Luke.
22. Padmé used a hidden key to unlock her handcuffs, Obi-Wan's chain was broken by the thrust of the Acklay (crab creature), and Anakin wrapped his chain around the horn of the Reek, which reared back and snapped the chain.
23. 5
24. Yoda said, "Begun the Clone War has."
25. Episode (or, if you think that answer was unfair, try War!)
26. Early in AOC, Organa, who was a Senator from Alderaan, said, "Do you think that is a wise decision during these stressful times?"
27. Commander Gree
28. Palpatine. Anakin cut off his arm, but Palpatine used blue Force lightning to flingMace out the window.
29. Cody
30. He was Captain Antilles, and he was the first person killed in ANH by Darth Vader by being lifted a foot off the ground, strangled, and thrown aside.
31. "I love?.?.?."
32. "I hate you!" was directed at his master, Obi-Wan. ROS

Princess Leia

1. Holding a blaster, preparing to fire at Imperial troops invading her ship.
2. Tantive IV was its name, CR90 Corvette was the make and model, and it was a Rebel blockade runner.

3. Technically at birth but, as an adult, he first saw Leia as a holo-gram projected by R2-D2 on Tatooine.
4. "Darth Vader, only you could be so bold." ANH
5. Several transmissions from Rebel spies were tracked to her ship.
6. To Leia's father on Alderaan
7. Detention block AA-23
8. "Aren't you a little short for a stormtrooper?"
9. His Serene Highness, Prince Bail Organa, First Chairman and Viceroy of Alderaan
10. "Looks like you managed to cut off our only escape route."
11. "Maybe you'd like it better in your cell, Your Highness."
12. "Into the garbage chute, flyboy."
13. "Put that thing away! You're going to get us all killed."
14. General Jan Dodonna
15. 19
16. A Wookiee
17. A laser brain
18. Stuck up?.?.?.?half-witted?.?.?.?scruffy-looking?.?.?.?nerf-herder. (Han took offense to "scruffy looking.")
19. An explosion caused an avalanche in the tunnels, blocking access to her ship.
20. She called him a scoundrel, and he said he liked the sound of that. ESB
21. Welding a part of the Millennium Falcon
22. "Don't! It's a trap!"
23. Lando
24. R2-D2 zapped the chain with a blue laser.
25. On Luke's advice, she jammed their comlinks by using the cen-ter switch on her bike's control panel.

26. "Cut it out!"
27. Images of her being beautiful, kind, and sad. It's a matter of intense debate how she could remember a woman she only saw at childbirth.
28. Leia Amidala Skywalker
29. Leia called it a power she didn't understand and she could never have.
30. A bridge among the trees on Endor
31. When Imperial stormtroopers had captured Han and Leia, and Han realized Leia had a blaster ready.
32. One: Carrie Fisher. The baby Leia in ROS was played by Aiden Barton, the son of editor Roger Barton.
33. Totally

Qui-Gon Jinn

1. Kwy-Gawn
2. "Captain." It was said off-screen to a pilot as he and Obi-Wan approached Naboo.
3. "Anakin! Anakin! No!" was heard as Yoda meditated and Anakin killed the Tusken Raiders in their camp.
4. "I don't sense anything."
5. A series of laser gates, which were red force fields that opened and closed sporadically.
6. 20,000 Republic dactaries
7. Watto was a Toydarian, and mind tricks don't work on him, only money.
8. "There's something about this boy."

9. Qui-Gon took a sample from young Anakin to determine his midi-chlorian count.
10. He bet with Watto that Anakin would win the pod race.
11. How to return from the dead with his spirit intact
12. Fear, especially for something that was as trivial as a trade dispute
13. Dioxin
14. Pallies
15. Jedi reflexes
16. By grabbing Jar Jar's tongue in a display of Jedi reflexes
17. His ship
18. Before the suns set
19. Qui-Gon bet the podracer against Anakin's freedom that Sebulba would lose.
20. Qui-Gon used the Force to ensure the cube came up blue, the color that represented Anakin.
21. Obi-Wan flew close by with the Naboo ship and Qui-Gon leapt up several feet onto the entrance ramp before the ship sped off.
22. In the cockpit of a Naboo spacecraft
23. He knelt and waited for the force field to deactivate again.
24. Darth Maul gave Qui-Gon an uppercut to the chin with the handle of his lightsaber, which momentarily stunned the Jedi knight.
25. In AOC, Qui-Gon was described as having been Dooku's apprentice when Dooku was a Jedi Knight.

R2-D2

1. In Anakin Skywalker's childhood bedroom. TPM
2. He repaired the shield generators on the outside of Padmé's spacecraft, under direct enemy fire, by bypassing the ship's main power drive.
3. They were droids.
4. Captain Antilles
5. The motivator
6. Carbon scoring
7. The restraining bolt was short-circuiting his recording system.
8. Lying down sideways
9. The Death Star's technical plans
10. There was a small hit to repair, and a stabilizer needed to be locked down.
11. His circuits or gears
12. Thermal
13. 725 to 1
14. The droids, R2-D2 and C-3PO.
15. On the master's (Jabba's) sail barge. ROJ
16. Serve drinks. ROJ
17. R2-D2 got hit by a blaster and malfunctioned.
18. Rocket jets appeared near R2-D2's legs, and he took flight for the first time onscreen.
19. Hit the center eye.
20. On the observation platform at the top of the ship's spire.
21. He squirted them with oil and then set them on fire with his jet thrusters.
22. Five. Only ROS didn't.

23. The droid kicked R2-D2 over.
24. In all six. A partial list: ANH: stopped the trash compactor. ESB: fixed the hyperdrive. ROJ: passed lightsaber to Luke. TPM: fixed Nubian ship's shield. AOC: stopped factory from pouring hot steel on Padmé. ROS: Sent elevator to save Anakin and Obi-Wan. And much, much more!

The Rebel Alliance

1. Captain Antilles
2. Gold and Red
3. General Jan Dodonna
4. He said that R2-D2 looked beat up.
5. Tiree and Hutch
6. Biggs Darklighter
7. Eject!
8. About twenty guns. Some on the surface, some on the towers.
9. Biggs Darklighter.
10. "Wait!" Then he was shot down by Darth Vader, of all people.
11. 15 minutes.
12. "I'm all right." Then his X-Wing fighter exploded and he wasn't.
13. Luke Skywalker
14. Echo Seven
15. General Carlist Rieekan
16. Dack Ralter
17. Major
18. Outside the base's Zone 12, and moving east
19. 1

20. Luke Skywalker
21. Echo Base
22. A death mark (or death threat); in this case, one from Jabba the Hutt.
23. The first marker
24. Rogue Two was the call signal for Zev, the snowspeeder pilot.
25. "Headquarters personnel, report to command center."
26. Station 38
27. It meant they'd been discovered by the Empire and needed to evacuate Hoth immediately.
28. A fleet of Star Destroyers
29. Two
30. An ion cannon
31. Attack pattern delta
32. Harpoons and tow cables
33. He got hit by a blast and died.
34. Wedge Antilles
35. Bothan spies
36. The location of the second Death Star, and that the weapons system was not yet functional.
37. The Death Star's protective energy shield had to be deactivated before an attack.
38. They disguised it as a cargo ship and used a secret Imperial clearance code to get landing rights.
39. The main reactor
40. Camouflage (It was evidently deemed more necessary on them than on a shiny gold droid.)
41. He stole an Imperial speeder bike and the troops gave chase.
42. The Emperor allowed them to know.
43. Gray and green

44. To holding sector MV-7
45. The SuperStar Destroyer, the Imperial fleet's command ship
46. Wedge Antilles
47. Three

The Ships

1. Eleven
2. Have it destroyed.
3. Thirty
4. An unexpected blast from the Millennium Falcon
5. Six
6. It had curved wings.
7. "Lock S-foils in attack position."
8. Two X-Wing fighters, one Y-Wing fighter, and the Millennium Falcon
9. Four
10. Three
11. Two
12. The second Death Star
13. Darth Vader's
14. PT 321. For the record, the ship was an Imperial Lambda-class shuttle.
15. His father's Imperial Lambda-class shuttle
16. Tydirium
17. Han and Chewbacca's Millennium Falcon, piloted by ex-owner Lando Calrissian and Nien Nunb, the alien from Sullustan
18. The medical frigate
19. Star Destroyers

20. Lando's (or, rather Han's) Millennium Falcon emerged from the explosion with a loud "Woo-Hoo!" from its pilot.
21. When Qui-Gon showed a hologram of it to Watto.
22. 3
23. The hyperdrive was leaking.
24. The ship was a J-type 327 Nubian. The parts list was stored in R2-D2.
25. A propeller airplane
26. The five other films each began with a single large ship passing by.
27. "Fire the emergency booster engines!"
28. Fire ships, acting as giant fire extinguishers.
29. The hyperspace transport ring allowed hyperspace (faster-than-light) travel for ships that didn't have a hyperdrive of their own.
30. General Grievous's
31. General Dooku's command ship was a Trade Federation cruiser.
32. A Naboo Skiff
33. Eleven
34. It's the same corridor from the same Alderaan starcruiser (later called a blockade runner) that Darth Vader boarded in the first scene of ANH.

Special Effects

1. The shot in the beginning where the escape pod with C-3PO and R2-D2 moves away from Princess Leia's ship.
2. Broomsticks. The broomsticks were replaced by glowing colors during post-production.

3. It was all done with mirrors. Mirrors covered the wheels of the speeder, reflected the sand below, and gave the appearance of flight.
4. It was destroyed in a triple explosion.
5. A broken air conditioner.
6. ANH was shot by mainly using vintage 1950s VistaVision cameras, not to save money, but the results were higher quality than newer 1970s cameras available.
7. THX
8. Instead of red lines, it appeared as blue circles.
9. By striking a suspension wire on the first Severn Bridge in Bristol, England. Shorter twangs were used for blasters; longer twangs for the ships.
10. When Vader/Anakin died at the end of ROJ.
11. A microphone was put inside the regulator of a scuba tank.
12. An elephant's scream was combined with the sound of a car moving on wet pavement.
13. Cardboard cutouts
14. ROJ: 25% was built. ANH: 50% was built. ESB: 100% was built. It was 80 feet long, with a diameter of 65 feet and a height of 16 feet.
15. Mark Hamill threw the lightsaber into the snowbank, and the scene was run in reverse.
16. A potato
17. It was (reportedly) the sound of several Alcatraz cell doors shutting at the same time.
18. Eight. Two held Kenny Baker, three were remote control units, and three were built to be damaged onscreen.
19. An electric car window

20. A number of the models
21. Richard Marquand, the director
22. A dachsund
23. He recorded his hands squishing through a cheese casserole.
24. Bright red
25. A camera operator walked through the forest naturally, with the camera set to film at one frame per second. Once the footage was played at 24 frames per second, it appeared to be incredibly fast.
26. A sneaker appeared as a space ship in the top left of the screen.
27. A human skull. It appeared for only a few frames.
28. A great electric blue flame
29. The weakened breathing sound was originally intended for Vader's breathing in ANH, but was replaced by a "healthier" sounding effect.
30. It's the first theatrical Hollywood film to be shot completely with a high-definition digital camera.
31. Nothing. Just prior to the guitar-chord explosion, there was a moment of total silence.
32. In most shots during the lightsaber duel, Lee provided the face, and computer graphics experts added it to a stunt double's body.
33. The San Francisco 49ers
34. You type it all with your left hand.

Tatooine

1. The planet that it's farthest from.
2. Five: all but ESB. In ROS, it was in the final scene.
3. In the outer rim
4. A long, serpentine skeleton
5. Banthas
6. Anchorhead
7. The binary language of moisture vaporators and Bocce
8. The south range
9. Tusken Raiders
10. Two
11. In twelve systems
12. The XP-38. Luke had a mere XP-34.
13. The Jundland Wastes were the part of Tatooine where the Tusken Raiders assaulted Luke. Obi-Wan said they were not to be traveled lightly.
14. In the Dune Sea of Tatooine
15. The Pit of Carkoon
16. Over a thousand years
17. It's small, out of the way, poor?.?.?.? it was controlled by the Hutts?.?.?.? and the Hutts weren't looking for Queen Amidala.
18. They had transmitters hidden on their bodies, and if an escape was attempted, said Anakin, "they blow you up!"
19. Mos Espe
20. About halfway home, according to the tracks.
21. A Jawa standing outside its Jawa sandcrawler.

The Technology

1. A giant vacuum hose
2. A T-16, also known as a Skyhopper
3. Proton torpedoes
4. The blast points on their sandcrawler were too accurate.
5. The mind probe
6. No life forms were registered by Imperial scanners.
7. It was attached to his belt.
8. They found footprints, and a circular metal ring that one of the droids dropped.
9. It was a big rectangular box, about the dimensions of a steamer trunk.
10. Binders, a form of handcuffs
11. Angle them
12. White (with black highlights)
13. The turbo-lasers
14. Five
15. When Han fired on it, the droid's self-destruct mechanism engaged.
16. A medical droid. the scene took place in Luke's recovery room.
17. Through a Rebel officer's electrobinoculars.
18. Four
19. An energy binder
20. Energy balls
21. TC-14
22. Droidekas
23. T-14. But buying a new ship would be cheaper.
24. The pod from 2001: A Space Odyssey
25. A mobile projector, walking on four spindly spider legs.

26. Yellow with green details
27. A toxic Kamino saberdart was fired by Jango Fett.
28. Three
29. Arfour (full name: R4-P17) was an astromech droid. It accompanied Obi-Wan on his Delta-7 Aethersprite-class starfighter, and on his Eta-2 Actis-class interceptor. The R4 was said to be an improvement on the earlier R2 units.
30. A flying chopper motorcycle without wheels. Technically, it was one of many types of speeder bike.
31. A broken shifter
32. Buzz droids
33. 3224.
34. Ray shields

Who Did That?

1. Luke Skywalker, Anakin Skywalker (twice), Mace Windu, and Count Dooku
2. To Padmé in ROS, and to Luke in ESB
3. Luke in ANH, Anakin in AOC, and Beru and Owen at the end of ROS
4. Red Five
5. Obi-Wan laid healing hands on Grandmother (Padmé) in ROS, and grandchild (Luke) in ANH.
6. Obi-Wan convinced Vader to release Padmé in ROS, and Grand Moff Tarkin told Vader to stop choking Motti in ANH.
7. Yes, but only if you consider the halving of Darth Maul to qualify as an amputation.
8. Only one. When Anakin and Obi-Wan duelled in ROS, they each had a blue lightsaber.

9. Luke, Leia, Chewbacca, Darth Vader (arguably) and, if you look in the last Empire scene in ROS, you can see a younger Tarkin with the Emperor and Vader.

10. Anakin Skywalker, Obi-Wan Kenobi, R2-D2, and C-3PO. The Emperor was named but didn't appear in ANH.

11. ROS had five: The losers were Count Dooku, Grievous, Mace Windu and other Jedi, Yoda, and Anakin.

12. George Lucas, who had a cold during shooting. ROS

13. In ANH, good guy Obi-Wan had a blue lightsaber, and bad guy Vader's was red.

14. ROJ

15. In ROJ, Vader held Luke's saber.

16. Chewbacca. In the end of ANH, he stood behind Han and Luke, but was not given a like medal for bravery or heroism .

17. Han Solo, while evading Imperial fighters in ESB.

18. Leia, the daughter of Anakin Skywalker, almost always hit her target. The Force was with her indeed.

19. Qui-Gon spoke during Yoda's meditation in AOC.

20. Luke, Leia, Han, Chewbacca, Lando, R2-D2, C-3PO, and three Ewoks

Who Said That?

1. Han Solo said it in ANH just before rescuing Leia, and Anakin said it in ROS just before rescuing Palpatine.

2. In ROJ, Chewbacca and some Ewoks swing to an Imperial vehicle, and in ROS, Wookiees swing toward the enemy in the Battle of Kashyyyk.

3. C-3PO, and interestingly, it was spoken on the same ship: Bail Organa's Tantive IV.
4. Luke, as the Millennium Falcon approached the Death Star for the first time; and Han, in the garbage compactor.
5. Leia, inside the space worm while hiding on the asteroid.
6. C-3PO, inside Jabba's palace; and Han, while about to be cooked on an Ewok campfire.
7. Obi-Wan, aboard the Neimoidian ship.
8. Anakin, inside the arena on Geonosis.
9. Anakin, as a blast door was closing on General Grievous's ship.
10. Lando, regarding his ever-changing arrangement with Darth Vader in ESB.
11. C-3PO to Chewbacca as the Wookiee was repairing him on the Cloud City. ESB.
12. Qui-Gon to Obi-Wan aboard the Trade Federation ship at the beginning of TPM.
13. Darth Vader, just before admitting to being Luke's father in ESB.
14. Palpatine, in AOC, before he destroyed both.
15. Jango Fett said that as he first met Obi-Wan Kenobi in AOC.
16. Obi-Wan to Anakin in AOC
17. Qui-Gon to Jar Jar as they meet on Naboo. TPM
18. Young Anakin in TPM
19. Han to Leia just after they plunged into the garbage compactor in ANH.
20. Han Solo in ANH
21. Luke, just before the Battle of Yavin, in ANH.

Yoda

1. From Obi-Wan's Force ghost on Hoth
2. "Feel like what?"
3. "Wars not make one great."
4. Come to Yoda's home and eat.
5. Root leaf
6. "How you get so big eating food of this kind?"
7. "The boy has no patience."
8. Luke was not focused on the present, he was reckless, and he was too old.
9. "Concentrate!"
10. Anger, fear, and aggression
11. 800 years
12. Sick, old, and weak
13. 900
14. "Strong am I with the Force, but not that strong."
15. Once Luke confronted Vader, a Jedi would he be.
16. "Forever will it dominate your destiny."
17. That Anakin was in terrible pain.
18. Sector 5-1-5.
19. Six. Three on each hand. The number of toes, however, had been a matter that changed from film to film.
20. Green
21. AOC
22. Yoda converted it into a ball that was returned to Dooku before it careened off a wall and burst into flames.
23. Count Dooku
24. The path to the dark side

25. "Train yourself to let go of everything you fear to lose."
26. Yoda threw his lightsaber into an opponent, impaling him, and then retrieved it from the opponent's body to continue fighting others.
27. "Gone he is. Consumed by Darth Vader."
28. "Misplaced may be."
29. His cloak
30. Albert Einstein
31. "There is another Skywalker."
32. R2-D2 beeped